PREFACE

When Luke wrote the message of the gospel to Theophilus, he declared that his desire was to set forth, in order, a declaration of those things that are most surely believed among us. Luke desired that Theophilus might know the certainty of those things in which he had been instructed.

We seem to be living in a day of spiritual confusion. Paul wrote to the Ephesians that they not be as children, tossed to and fro with every wind of doctrine by the slight of men and the cunning craftiness whereby they lie in wait to deceive. Because of all the confusion in the church today, and the many winds of doctrine that continue to blow through the body of Christ, we felt that it would be good to have various pastors write booklets that would

1

address the issues and give to you the solid biblical basis of what we believe and why we believe it.

Our purpose is that the spiritual house that you build will be set upon the solid foundation of the eternal Word of God, thus we know that it can withstand the fiercest storms.

Pastor Chuck Smith
Calvary Chapel of Costa Mesa, California

THE
AFTERGLOW

by Henry Gainey

P.O. Box 8000, Costa Mesa, CA 92628

The Afterglow
by Henry Gainey
General Editor: Chuck Smith

Published by **The Word For Today**

P.O. Box 8000 Costa Mesa CA 92628

© 1998 The Word For Today

ISBN 0–936728–76-6

Unless otherwise indicated, Scripture quotations in this book are taken from the King James Version of the Bible.

TABLE OF CONTENTS

Introduction

This book is written for pastors and for the body of Christ in general. Its purpose is to give instruction in conducting "Believer's Meetings" and "Afterglow Services."

Many Christians are rightfully concerned about the proper use of the gifts of the Holy Spirit in the Church today. Unscriptural practices, especially in some highly visible churches on television, have confused the body of Christ and caused many godly people who know the Scriptures to shy away from the use of the gifts. This should not be.

Jesus said we would receive His power when the Holy Spirit came upon us. The gifts of the Holy Spirit are the manifestation of His power. If we learn to operate the gifts in a scriptural manner, decently and in order (1 Corinthians 14:40), we can begin to experience the true power of the early church, the dynamic power of Jesus Christ through the Holy Spirit.

CHAPTER 1
DECENTLY AND IN ORDER

Calvary Chapel Statement of Faith Regarding the Baptism and Gifts of the Holy Spirit

"After Jesus ascended to heaven, He poured out His Holy Spirit on the believers in Jerusalem, enabling them to fulfill His command to preach the Gospel to the entire world, an obligation shared by all believers today.

We believe in the gifts of the Holy Spirit mentioned in the Scriptures, and that they are valid for today if they are exercised within the scriptural guidelines. We as believers are to covet the best gifts, seeking to exercise them in love that the whole body of Christ might be edified. We believe that love is more important

5

than the most spectacular gifts, and without this love all exercise of spiritual gifts is worthless.

We reject…the over-emphasis of spiritual gifts, experiential signs and wonders to the exclusion of biblical Teaching.

In our services, we focus on a personal relationship with God through worship, prayer, and the teaching of the Word of God. We teach both expositionally and topically. We do not allow speaking in tongues loudly during services, nor prophecy while a Bible study is in progress because we do not believe that the Holy Spirit would interrupt Himself. We have specific 'Afterglow Services' and Believer's Meetings when these gifts of the Spirit may be exercised."[1]

The Nature of the Holy Spirit

The Holy Spirit is a person, the third person of the trinity, the Godhead, which is made up of God the Father, God the Son, and God the Holy Spirit. A common misconception is that the Holy

---

[1].   Calvary Chapel Statement of Faith, from *What Calvary Chapel Teaches*, by Larry Taylor (Twin Peaks, CA: Calvary Chapel Bible College) pp 10–11.

Spirit is merely a force. The Holy Spirit is God. Many Scriptures speak of the personality of the Holy Spirit. For instance, we can grieve the Holy Spirit (Ephesians 4:30). We cannot grieve a force. We can only grieve a person with feelings. We can quench the Spirit (1 Thessalonians 5:19). If we can quench him, He must have a plan, a will, which we can disobey. We can lie to the Holy Spirit. Ananias and Sapphira did in Acts 5, and both fell down dead.

The Holy Spirit is first mentioned by name in Genesis 1:2, where He acts. It says, "And the Spirit of God (the Holy Spirit) moved upon the face of the waters." He is last mentioned by name in the closing verses of Revelation, where He speaks: "And the Spirit and the bride say, Come" (Revelation 22:17). He appears throughout Scripture as a person, speaking, acting, empowering, saving, filling, working on the behalf of God's people. He works in us, and through us. The third person of the Godhead is indeed, a real person, and not a mere force.

What Are Afterglow Services and Believer's Meetings?

A "Believer's Meeting" is a special meeting of the body of Christ in which the spoken gifts of the Holy Spirit such as tongues, the interpretation of tongues, and prophecy are exercised in the meeting, according to the scriptural guidelines that are outlined in 1 Corinthians 14.

> *How is it then, brethren? When ye come together, every one of you hath a **psalm**, hath a **doctrine**, hath a **tongue**, hath a **revelation**, hath an **interpretation**. Let all things be done unto edifying (1 Corinthians 14:26, emphasis added).*

In most church services, we have singing of psalms and teaching of doctrine. The addition of tongues, the interpretation of tongues, and prophetic revelations distinguish a "Believer's Meeting" from a regular church service. Most churches do not operate these gifts in their regular meetings.

An Afterglow Service is an abbreviated version of a Believer's Meeting. It is generally conducted after a regular church service, but "afterglow" does not mean that it is "after" another service. Afterglow refers to the Shekinah glory of the Lord. Moses said to God, "I beseech thee, show me thy **glory**" (Exodus 33:18).

*[The Lord answered], I will make all **my goodness** pass before thee, and I will proclaim the name of the* LORD *before thee; and will be **gracious** to whom I will be gracious, and will show **mercy** on whom I will show mercy. And he said, Thou canst not see my face: for there shall no man see me, and live. And the* LORD *said, Behold, there is a place by me, and thou shalt stand upon a rock: and it shall come to pass, while **my glory** passeth by, that I will put thee in a cleft of the rock, and will cover thee with my hand while I pass by: And I will take away mine hand, and **thou shalt see my back parts** (afterglow): but my face shall not be seen (Exodus 33:19–23, emphasis added).*

An Afterglow Service is a special time of waiting on the Lord to see and experience His glory in the ministry of the gifts of the Holy Spirit. When we see His glory, we will also witness His goodness, His grace, and His great mercy on us. Part of the "Believer's Meeting" then, is actually an "afterglow" service. That which makes the Believer's Meeting different from other church services is the afterglow portion of the meeting.

In summary, a Believer's Meeting consists of:

1) Singing

2) Teaching of doctrine

3) Tongues

4) Interpretation of tongues

5) Prophetic revelations

An Afterglow consists of:

1) Tongues

2) Interpretation of tongues

3) Prophetic revelations

Many Afterglow Services begin with singing, and the leader often gives a brief exposition of Scripture concerning the baptism and gifts of the Spirit, and then moves into the use of the gifts. This is essentially the same as a "Believer's Meeting," so many times the terms "afterglow" and "Believer's Meeting" are used interchangeably.

Afterglows are less formal than regular church services and usually involve more direct participation of the body of Christ. Several people may speak in tongues, several may interpret, and several may prophesy. All this should be done in accordance with Scripture under the guidance of the Holy Spirit. The leader must be sensitive to the Holy Spirit and is responsible for conducting the meeting and seeing that all things are done decently and in order (1 Corinthians 14:40). His guide is the Word of God, especially 1 Corinthians 14. The leader should be intimately familiar with this portion of Scripture and its guidelines for the use of the spoken gifts.

Some teach that a "Believer's Meeting" is a meeting in which we operate the gifts of the Holy Spirit. That is true, but we must not assume the gifts are not in operation in a regular church service. The gift of teaching (Romans 12:7), operated in a regular service, is a very powerful gift of the Holy Spirit. Singing and making melody in our hearts to the Lord (Ephesians 5:19) is certainly also the operation of the Holy Spirit. Occasionally even the gifts of prophecy, word of wisdom and word of knowledge may come forth from the pastor as he is teaching and leading the service. But a regular service would not usually include these gifts from others in the congregation.

The gifts that define a "Believer's Meeting" then are generally tongues, interpretation of tongues, and prophecy. In the portion of the meeting in which these gifts are exercised, there is often a time of "waiting on the Lord" to speak to us through other members of the body with the gifts. Someone may speak in tongues; someone else may give the interpretation; someone then may prophesy. As we begin to move in this supernatural realm and trust God to speak to us, the Lord will frequently minister with other gifts of the Spirit. Sometimes God will begin to touch the sick, and people may be spontaneously healed. The Lord may speak through a "word of knowledge" about a particular problem in someone's life that He wants to resolve. My wife, for instance, was delivered from smoking cigarettes in a Believer's Meeting through a word of knowledge.

In the context of 1 Corinthians 14, these gifts were operated by the believers in Christ in the presence of believers who were familiar with the gifts. Strict guidelines were given, lest an unbeliever or a believer unfamiliar with the use of these gifts think they were insane. Church services were not designed to be secret meetings, or to exclude people, so occasionally unbelievers or untaught believers would witness the operation of these gifts.

What About Tongues?

Tongues often becomes a big issue when churches begin to get interested in the baptism of the Holy Spirit, the gifts and their manifestations. Unfortunately, those that have the gift of tongues often get divided from those who do not. There are several reasons this happens:

1. Those who receive tongues may get proud, thinking they are super-spiritual, not realizing that tongues is a gift from God. That spiritual pride offends those who do not have the gift.

2. Many have been taught against tongues repeatedly over the years. It may take awhile for them to put aside erroneous teaching and take the Bible at its word.

3. Many have witnessed the abuse and misuse of tongues and are rightfully concerned about the use of this gift in their church.

The love of Jesus is needed in these situations to prevent problems and misunderstandings.

Not All Speak With Tongues

Some teach that when you are baptized with the Holy Spirit, you must receive the gift of tongues. Although most people who receive the baptism do eventually receive tongues, it is unscriptural to teach that you must speak in tongues to receive the baptism of the Holy Spirit.

"Do all speak with tongues?" (1 Corinthians 12:30). No. The baptism is received by faith. The Scriptures do not require any physical sign such as tongues to validate that the Spirit has indeed bestowed the baptism of the Holy Spirit upon the believer. I know several godly, spirit-filled people who have not received the gift of tongues. And I know several ungodly, backslidden Christians who have the gift. Speaking in tongues does not make a person more spiritual than the one who does not speak in tongues, and is not a valid measure of spirituality. Preoccupation with tongues as a spiritual barometer is unscriptural, and unkind.

Having said that, tongues, however, often seems to be the hurdle that many people have to get over to enter the doorway into receiving other gifts. Even if they do not receive tongues, they must at least accept the fact that tongues and the other gifts are valid and are for today. Once they believe that God still moves in the supernatural realm, they are usually open to receiving other gifts. Many will then receive prophecy, word of wisdom, or word of knowledge. Sometimes God will give them tongues later. Others, though, never receive tongues. It should not be a big deal or a point of contention. My mother was baptized with the Holy Spirit several years ago. I have seen many beautiful gifts of the Spirit manifest themselves in her life. She has the gift of mercy and she has a very powerful intercessory prayer ministry. Although she has prayed for tongues several times, she has never received the gift. Does God love her less than He loves me, since I have tongues? Of course not. For some reason, God decided my mother did not need that gift, but He has given her other beautiful gifts.

An advantage in receiving the baptism of the Holy Spirit and the gifts of the Spirit in a Believer's type service at your own church is that you are likely to know those who are ministering and trust them in this area. Receiving from the Lord in a protected, secure environment helps us to enter into the use of the gifts.

The church at Corinth was a gifted church, moving in and using the gifts of the Holy Spirit. Paul wrote to give them guidance in the use of the gifts. Some of the gifts were being abused.

> *If therefore the whole church be come together in one place, and all speak with tongues, and there come in those that are unlearned, or unbelievers, will they not say ye are mad? (1 Corinthians 14:23).*

If everyone is speaking in tongues, the untaught, or unbelievers will think you are crazy. Paul told them only two or three should speak in tongues, and only two or three should prophesy. In their services Paul allowed for some use of these spoken gifts. Was this a unique case for Corinth? Should tongues be allowed in church services today? The key to this appears to be the presence of the untaught, or unbelievers. If they are present, the use of tongues should be discouraged. That is why most Calvary Chapels do not permit the use of tongues in their general services.

Years ago, Calvary Chapel of Costa Mesa recognized a need for the expression of these gifts in the church, and began having special services in which it was announced that these gifts would be in operation. These were "Afterglows," or "Believer's Meetings." They continue to have these meetings today, and those who attend come expecting the use of the spoken gifts. Therefore, they would not be offended or think those using the gifts were insane.

Although there was a problem with carnality at Corinth, we do not believe Paul's instructions to them regarding tongues is making allowance for a special case of out of control carnal Christians who just have to speak in tongues. Quite the opposite. Paul said, "I thank my God, I speak with tongues more than ye all" (1 Corinthians 14:18). His instructions put the proper limitations on the use of the gift.

As we shall see later, the use of the gift of speaking in tongues is primarily for our private prayer life.

I led "Believer's Meetings" at Calvary Chapel, Costa Mesa from 1976 to 1979. In recent years I have attended Calvary Chapel of Tallahassee, and continue to lead "Believer's Meetings" there about once every two months.

Calvary Chapel Tallahassee Guidelines

Pastor Kent Nottingham of Calvary Chapel, Tallahassee, invites the people to a Believer's Service with the following written information and guidelines:

"A 'Believer's Service' is a special service for the exercise of the spiritual gifts (1 Corinthians 12–14). The 'gifts,' generally speaking, are for the edification of believers in the body of Christ. At Calvary Chapel, the exercise of vocal gifts—such as tongues, interpretation and prophecy—are not encouraged during our regular Sunday morning or Wednesday evening services. The biblical basis for this practice can be found in 1 Corinthians 14:23. Unbelievers visiting the church may not receive the gospel after seeing what they perceive to be insane or strange practices." He goes on to say: "We design our Believer's Services to be a separate time of experiencing the love and power of Jesus Christ, in decency and order (1 Corinthians 14:32–33). Those from very conservative backgrounds will find that the service is anything but insane or strange, and they will be pleased to discover the blessings that accompany the working of the Holy Spirit.

Those from very Pentecostal backgrounds will experience the gentleness of the Holy Spirit administered within the confines and balance of the Word of God."

Should Our Church Have a Believer's Meeting or an Afterglow Service?

Should our church have a "Believer's Meeting" or an "Afterglow Service?" A better question might be, "Does *God* want us to have one?" I do not know the answer to that question, but I do know that Jesus commanded His disciples to wait in Jerusalem "for the promise of the Father, which, saith he, ye have heard of (from) me. For John truly baptized with water; but ye shall be baptized with the Holy Ghost not many days hence" (Acts 1:4–5). Paul the apostle said to "covet earnestly the best gifts" (1 Corinthians 12:31). One way to obey Scripture and receive the baptism and gifts of the Holy Spirit is through an Afterglow Service, or a Believer's Meeting.

We have found that a Believer's Meeting is a good time to teach about the baptism of the Holy Spirit and offer to pray for and lay hands on those who would like to receive it. Jesus said we would receive His power when the Holy

Spirit came upon us (Acts 1:8). That power is given that we might be His witnesses. That power is given through the gifts of the Holy Spirit. Just as the baptism of the Holy Spirit and tongues were first manifested on the day of Pentecost, the baptism of the Holy Spirit continues to be the portal of entry into tongues and the other gifts of the Spirit. Therefore most Calvary Chapels start Afterglow Services to minister the baptism of the Holy Spirit to the believers and to help get them involved in and familiar with the use of the gifts of the spirit.

When I was baptized with the Holy Spirit in 1971, I found there was something even more important than the power I received when the Spirit came upon me. I began to experience an intimacy with Jesus Christ that I had never known before. His Word became especially precious to me. I could not get enough of reading the Bible, and for the first time, I really understood it. I could feel His presence with me. I had a hunger and a thirst for God as never before. I became aware of His leading in my life. I knew I was no longer alone.

In my new-found deep communion with God, I knew I was fulfilling the purpose for which He created me: to have fellowship with Him. "God is faithful, by whom ye were called unto the fellowship of his Son Jesus Christ our Lord" (1 Corinthians 1:9). That fellowship was glorious. Though I had been saved for years, for the first time I knew real joy. His love overflowed me, and I experienced His "peace that passeth understanding" (Philippians 4:7). I *knew* that I knew Him, and that I was eternally saved! I knew that Jesus loved me, and I loved Him with all my heart. I was radically changed. From that time forward, I knew that Christ was to be the center of my life. Knowing Jesus became the most precious thing in my life. It still is.

Since that time I have had a burden for souls. My first burden is to bring them to Christ for salvation, then to minister the baptism of the Holy Spirit to them that they might know the joy and the love of God that I have known. What greater gift can God give someone? What greater honor can He bestow upon us, than to use us to bring others to Him?

Have you ever seen a couple in love? They can't take their eyes off one another. They can't quit talking to others about their beloved. God

gave us that kind of human love that we might
have a glimpse into the realm of His agape love
for us. He can't take His eyes off us. He wants us
to love Him the same way He loves us. The
Holy Spirit is our teacher, our guide. He will
lead us into all truth. He will lead us into that
deep love relationship with Jesus Christ. Most
people say they came to know Jesus in a deeper,
more intimate way after they were baptized
with the Holy Spirit. To me, this is the greatest
reason for desiring it, for seeking it: that love
relationship with Jesus Christ.

In the setting of a Believer's Meeting, we can
learn about the baptism and the gifts of the
Spirit and how they operate. We can pray for
one another and minister to one another using
the gifts. Many hear the voice of God speaking
to them for the first time in a Believer's Meeting.
The gift of prophecy is especially used by God to
express His great love for us. He uses it for our
edification, exhortation, and *comfort* (1 Corinthians
14:3). As prophecies come forth from God's
saints, I often hear people weeping softly as God
touches hearts with His Word. Others may hear
tongues for the first time. When done decently
and in order with an interpretation, tongues can
truly be a blessing. Others may be healed, or

receive a word of wisdom or a word of knowledge from the Lord. A Believer's Meeting is a time of ministry, but it is also a time of learning. For ye may all prophesy one by one, that all may learn, and all may be comforted (1 Corinthians 14:31).

When I was in college I took a course in physics. During the lectures, certain concepts were presented that were difficult to understand. Abstract ideas frequently puzzled us. Then we had a laboratory time in which we did experiments which confirmed what we had learned in the textbooks. The lab experiments made it "real" to us. We moved from the abstract theory to the concrete application of knowledge. The material presented was no longer theory, but became reality as we verified it in the lab. So it is with the Holy Spirit. He wants to apply the truth of God and make it a reality in our lives as we experience it firsthand in the laboratory of life. We read about the gifts of the Spirit in Scripture, but the Holy Spirit wants to bestow those gifts upon us and teach us how to use them. He wants to empower us to minister to one another. He wants to empower us to bear the fruit of love. He wants us to experience His true agape love for us. Then He wants us to love Him with that agape love of Christ flowing through us back to Him. Finally, He wants us to love others in the same way.

The Bible is our manual about Emmanuel. The Holy Spirit takes the Word of God out of the classroom and into the laboratory of life, into the world in which we live.

When and How Do We Start an Afterglow?

Afterglow services can be started at any time in the life of a church. Many people that are born again, and that love the Lord, but have not been baptized with the Holy Spirit, realize that something is missing, that God has more for them. He created us with a void, that we might desire an intimacy with Him that only the Holy Spirit can give us. When the Apostle Paul came to Ephesus in Acts chapter nineteen, he saw something missing in certain disciples he found there. He asked them, "Have you received the Holy Spirit since you believed?" And they said unto him, "We have not so much as heard whether there be any Holy Ghost" (Acts 19:2). Then "when Paul had laid his hands upon them, the Holy Ghost came on them; and they spoke with tongues, and prophesied" (Acts 19:6). Like this group, many people will be open and receive immediately. Others will need some preparation. If they are totally unfamiliar with the baptism and gifts of the Spirit, they may not be receptive to this "new thing" until they have been taught about it from the Scriptures.

If you are teaching systematically through the Word, a good time to start would be right after a teaching on the baptism of the Holy Spirit or the gifts of the Spirit, such as Acts chapter one or two, or Romans twelve, or First Corinthians chapter twelve, thirteen, or fourteen.

Another way would be to announce that you are beginning a series of teachings on the baptism and gifts of the Spirit, and introduce the people in that way.

Responsible Christians first want to know that what is being taught is *scriptural* and that it is *for today*. With a group that is already convinced, an afterglow can be started very soon. With a hesitant group, the scriptural groundwork needs to be laid. In the next few sections, I will present some of that groundwork and try to answer some of the usual objections. I will discuss some of the gifts in detail, but will not attempt a comprehensive exposition of the gifts. For a more in-depth study of the baptism and gifts of the Holy Spirit, I recommend Pastor Chuck Smith's book, *Living Water*.[1]

---

[1]. *Living Water, The Power of the Holy Spirit in Your Life,* by Chuck Smith (The Word For Today),1996.

CHAPTER 2
BAPTISM OF THE HOLY SPIRIT

Introduction to the Baptism of the Holy Spirit

I indeed baptize you with water unto repentance: but he that cometh after me is mightier that I, whose shoes I am not worthy to bear: he shall baptize you with the Holy Ghost, and with fire (Matthew 3:11).

Important doctrines in Scripture are taught in several places. God wants to be sure we do not miss them. In all four gospels John the Baptist mentioned Jesus as the One coming who would baptize with the Holy Spirit. If a doctrine is mentioned in the gospels, occurs in the book of Acts and is taught in the epistles, we can rest assured that it is a proper practice for the church. Communion is a good example.

Scripture instructs us in all three of these areas regarding communion: Jesus instituted it with His disciples at the "Last Supper," it was practiced in Acts, and Paul taught on it in the epistles. The Bible also instructs us in all three areas regarding the baptism of the Holy Spirit. The baptism is mentioned in all four gospels, occurs on at least five occasions in the book of Acts, and is taught in the epistles.

Fulfillment of Pentecost

In Acts chapter two, He delivered on that promise to baptize them with the Holy Spirit:

And when the day of Pentecost was fully come, they were all with one accord in one place.

And suddenly there came a sound from heaven as of a rushing mighty wind, and it filled all the house where they were sitting.

And there appeared unto them cloven tongues like as of fire, and it sat upon each of them.

And they were all filled with the Holy Ghost, and began to speak with other tongues, as the Spirit gave them utterance.

And there were dwelling at Jerusalem Jews, devout men, out of every nation under heaven.

Now when this was noised abroad, the multitude came together, and were confounded, because that every man heard them speak in his own language.

And they were all amazed, and marveled, saying one to another, Behold, are not all these which speak Galileans?

And how hear we every man in our own tongue, wherein we were born?

Parthians, and Medes, and Elamites, and the dwellers in Mesopotamia, and in Judaea, and Cappadocia, in Pontus, and Asia,

Phrygia, and Pamphylia, in Egypt, and in the parts of Libya about Cyrene, and strangers of Rome, Jews and proselytes,

Cretes and Arabians, we do hear them speak in our tongues the wonderful works of God (Acts 2:1–11).

That first Pentecost after His resurrection, Jesus endued His followers with "power from on high." They were filled with the Holy Spirit, or "baptized" as Jesus had promised in Acts 1:5. This was then manifested by something that had never before happened in the history of the

world.[1] The disciples began speaking in
tongues, languages which they could not
understand, but which others who spoke the
languages could understand. The commotion
drew a large crowd and people from seventeen
different nations heard them speaking in their
own languages the wonderful works of God.
They were amazed. The men which were
speaking came from Galilee. Galileans were
generally uneducated and did not know foreign
languages. Truly this was a sign from God. Then
Peter, empowered by the Holy Spirit, preached
one of the mightiest sermons in Scripture and
three thousand people were saved that day.

The book of Acts records several other
instances of the baptism of the Holy Spirit after
that initial outpouring at Pentecost. Often the

---

[1]. All the other gifts of the Holy Spirit had previously been
manifested in the Old and New Testament Scriptures,
but tongues was brand new. The confounding of
languages by God at Babel was different from
tongues. At Babel, men began to speak new languages
which they understood. They forgot their old language
and could not communicate with one another. New
tongues at Babel were used to separate ungodly men.
New tongues at Pentecost were used to unite the body
of Christ.

laying on of hands is used to impart the "baptism" and the gifts. In Acts chapter eight, Philip went down and preached the gospel in Samaria. Many believed in Christ, but when Peter and John came down, "They laid their hands on them, and they received the Holy Ghost" (Acts 8:17). Paul was "filled with the Holy Ghost" (Acts 9:17) when Ananias laid hands on him. When Peter went to the House of Cornelius at Ceasarea and preached Christ unto them, "the Holy Ghost fell on all them which heard the word" (Acts 10:44). When Paul laid his hands on certain disciples at Ephesus, "the Holy Ghost came on them; and they spake with tongues, and prophesied" (Acts 19:6).

Supernatural Manifestations of the Baptism

We should expect supernatural manifestations when the baptism of the Holy Spirit is given, but we should not insist on them. When I lay hands on people to pray for them to receive the baptism, I pray for them to receive the gifts of the Spirit also. Many times they will receive the gift of tongues, sometimes they will prophesy, other times they will praise the Lord in English and sometimes "nothing" seems to happen. They may say, "Nothing happened, I don't feel any different. I didn't get tongues." I tell them what we "feel or experience" right now is not important. The baptism is received by faith, just as salvation is received by faith. Many who are saved have a dramatic emotional experience, accompanied by joy, weeping, or tremendous peace. Others who are saved often confess that they felt nothing at the time: no emotional experience. Those who "felt nothing" are just as saved as those who had a dramatic experience. I have seen a lot of fruit in the lives of Christians who initially "felt no different." We cannot go on feelings. Our feelings will deceive us. We must rely on facts and faith. The same is true with the baptism of the Holy Spirit and the gifts of the Spirit. They are received by faith, not blind faith, but faith based on fact. The fact is that Jesus promised salvation, the baptism of the Holy Spirit and the gifts of the Spirit to those who would come unto Him in faith, requesting them. Fact and faith are what is important. So I reassure them that when we pray for the baptism of the Holy Spirit in faith, that God gives it. Jesus said,

> *If ye then, being evil, know how to give good gifts*
> *unto your children: how much more shall your*

heavenly father give the Holy Spirit to them that ask him? (Luke 11:13).

God has promised to give it to us when we ask Him in faith. God keeps His Word. That is fact. We accept it on faith. "Feelings" and "experiences" will come later, just as the gifts will come later, if we remain open to receiving from God. If we go away disappointed that something "spectacular" did not happen, then we may indeed quench the Spirit and not move forward with God in all that He wants to do for us when we receive the baptism of the Holy Spirit.

The Baptism of the Holy Spirit Is Received Once

The baptism of the Holy Spirit is received once, by faith, just as salvation is received once, by faith. Jesus said, "ye shall be baptized with the Holy Ghost not many days hence" (Acts 1:5), indicating a single experience that would occur.

A Fresh Anointing of the Spirit

The book of Acts relates several occasions in which those who had already been baptized with the Holy Spirit received a fresh anointing of the Spirit.

Peter was brought before the Sanhedrin because of the healing of the lame man at the gate of the temple which is called beautiful. They asked,

> *By what power, or by what name, have ye done this? Then Peter, **filled with the Holy Ghost**, said unto them . . . by the name of Jesus Christ of Nazareth, whom ye crucified, whom God raised from the dead, even by him doth this man stand here before you whole (Acts 4:7–8, 10, emphasis added).*

When they were about to be released by the Sanhedrin, they were commanded not to speak at all nor teach in the name of Jesus (Acts 4:18). They returned to the body of believers and prayed that God would grant them boldness to speak His Word; that He would heal and that signs and wonders would "be done by the name of thy holy child Jesus. And when they had prayed, the place was shaken where they were assembled together; and *they were all filled with the Holy Ghost* and they spake the Word of God with boldness" (Acts 4:30–31, emphasis added).

When Ananias prayed for Saul (Paul) to receive his sight, he also prayed that he might be *"filled with the Holy Ghost"* (Acts 9:17). This was not a fresh anointing for Paul. This was his initial experience of the baptism of the Holy Spirit.

Later when Paul was in Cyprus, the deputy of the country, Sergius Paulus, "desired to hear the Word of God. But Elymas the sorcerer . . . withstood them, seeking to turn away the deputy from the faith. Then Saul (who is also called Paul) *filled with the Holy Ghost,* set his eyes on him" (Acts 13:7–9), and rebuking him, pronounced judgment upon him. He was immediately blinded. "Then the deputy, when he saw what was done, believed, being astonished at the doctrine of the Lord" (Acts 13:12).

In each of these instances in Acts, except when Paul was baptized with the Holy Spirit, they were filled with the Holy Spirit and received a fresh anointing of the Spirit when they were confronted by the enemies of the gospel. The Holy Spirit gave them boldness; He gave them power for signs and wonders; and He gave them joy when they were persecuted.

We Do Not Have to Tarry

Jesus told his disciples in Luke 24:49 to "tarry" in Jerusalem until they received power from on high. Today many teach that we must have "Tarrying Meetings" to receive the baptism of the Holy Spirit. After that initial outpouring of the Holy Spirit the day of Pentecost, there is no record in Scripture of believers having to wait, or "tarry" to receive the baptism. Initially, they were to tarry because the Lord was waiting for the day of Pentecost to pour out His Spirit in fulfillment of that feast time. After that there was no need to tarry. Certainly a meeting to receive the baptism of the Holy Spirit is desirable, but God does not require that we wait around all night to receive from Him. God is not reluctant. He wants to fill us. We receive the baptism of the Holy Spirit by faith, just as we are saved by faith. We cannot "earn" the baptism by tarrying. God bestows it freely on those who come to Him in faith.

CHAPTER 3
THE GIFTS OF THE SPIRIT

But the wise took oil in their vessels with their lamps (Matthew 25:4).

Now concerning spiritual gifts, brethren, I would not have you ignorant (1 Corinthians 12:1).

The Greek word for *gift*, as in "gift" of the Spirit, is *charisma*. It is derived from *charis*, the word for grace. Charisma is a gift of grace by God upon the church. In His goodness, He gives us the tools to minister to one another. For this reason, Christians with gifts of the Spirit are often called charismatic--a good thing to be. Unfortunately, because of the excesses of a few charismatic Christians, the word *charisma* has gotten a bad name in some Christian circles. This ought not to be. We should never bring reproach upon the name of Jesus Christ or upon the ministry of the Holy Spirit. Pastor Chuck Smith has written an excellent book showing the proper balance in the life of the believer with the baptism and gifts of the Spirit. It is entitled *Charisma vs. Charismania.*[1]

The church at Corinth was using the gifts of the Spirit, but there was ignorance in the church as to their proper use. Paul did not want them to be ignorant, just as the Lord does not want us to be ignorant today. It is possible to use a gift improperly.

> *Wherefore I give you to understand, that no man speaking by the Spirit of God calleth Jesus accursed: and that no man can say that Jesus is the Lord, but by the Holy Ghost (1 Corinthians 12:3).*

Apparently someone had been heard "speaking in tongues" and cursing Jesus. This attests to the fact that there are counterfeit

---

[1]. *Charisma vs. Charismania,* by Chuck Smith (Santa Ana, CA: The Word For Today Publishers), 1991.

tongues. Some cults today say they speak in tongues. Anyone speaking in an unknown tongue and cursing Jesus is not speaking true tongues motivated by the Holy Spirit. A believer witnessing false tongues might become afraid to seek the true gift of tongues, fearing that Satan could give him a counterfeit tongue. Today, even some churches teach that the gift of tongues is of the devil. This is unscriptural and wrong. If a believer is speaking in tongues and proclaiming Jesus as Lord, Paul tells us he is speaking by the Holy Spirit, not the devil. When we ask the Lord to give us this gift, we need not fear. Jesus said:

> *If ye then, being evil, know how to give good gifts unto your children: how much more shall your heavenly Father give the Holy Spirit to them that ask him (Luke 11:13).*

When a Spirit-filled believer in Jesus Christ comes to Him in faith asking for tongues or any other gift of the Spirit, Satan cannot give him a counterfeit gift.

Nine Gifts In 1 Corinthians Twelve

Paul mentions nine of the gifts in 1 Corinthians 12.

For to one is given by the Spirit the word of wisdom; to another the word of knowledge by the same Spirit; to another faith by the same Spirit; to another the gifts of healing by the same Spirit; to another the working of miracles; to another prophecy; to another discerning of spirits; to another divers (different) kinds of tongues; to another the interpretation of tongues (1 Corinthians 12:8–10).

To remember the nine gifts listed here, we might divide them into three groups of three. There are three revelation gifts, three power gifts, and three spoken gifts.

The Revelation Gifts

The three revelation gifts are word of wisdom, word of knowledge, and discerning of spirits. The Holy Spirit, through these gifts, supernaturally reveals information to us that we could not know otherwise.

Logos

The "word" in Greek is logos. *Logos* is not just a single word, but may embody a whole concept. The ultimate use of *logos* is in reference to Jesus: "In the beginning was the Word, and the Word was with God, and the Word was

God" (John 1:1). Here *logos,* the Word, is synonymous with Jesus Christ, the Word of God. It embodies all that Christ is: God in the flesh, who died on the cross for the sins of the world, who was raised from the dead on the third day, who is now ascended into heaven and sitting at the right hand of God the Father ever making intercession for us, and so much more!

Dr. A. E. Wilder-Smith told a story which helps to explain the concept of *logos.* Several years ago at Oxford, England, there was a debate between an evolutionist, Dr. Huxley, and a creationist, Dr. Wilberforce. Both were mathematicians. Dr. Huxley argued that with the "Probability Theory," a monkey typing at a typewriter for an infinite period of time would eventually type everything that could be written. He would type the sonnets of Shakespeare, and he would eventually type the 23d Psalm, the "Lord's Prayer," even the whole Bible. Huxley's idea of course, was to show that, given enough time, the molecules to produce life on the earth could eventually come together, and life could be produced by chance, just as Scripture could be produced by chance. Dr. Wilberforce was not able to overcome Huxley's logic and lost the debate. He was a broken man after that and never had another public debate about evolution. Dr. Wilder-Smith knew about the debate and knew something was wrong with Huxley's logic, but could not put his finger on it. He prayed for the answer for years. Then one day the answer came to him in a flash. He even described exactly what he was doing at that moment: walking in downtown Chicago, about to step up on a curb. Suddenly, it hit him. The biochemical reactions of life take place in water and are totally reversible. The molecules of amino acids would not stay together and keep adding amino acids until a protein was formed. As a matter of fact, the molecules of amino acids that form proteins are more likely to come apart from one another than they are to stay together. In the analogy of the monkey at the typewriter, this would amount to the letters coming back off the page shortly after they were typed. If that happened, the monkey would be lucky to ever type even a single word, much less anything of substance. This and much more was all revealed to Dr. Wilder-Smith in an instant of time. He said, "I could have written a whole book with the information I received instantaneously."

What happened? Dr. Wilder-Smith received the word of knowledge from the Lord. The concept of *logos* is demonstrated here. Suddenly he understood it all in an instant of time.

Word of Wisdom

The word of wisdom is *logos sophias, sophia* being the Greek for wisdom. Wisdom from God, like the other gifts, is supernatural wisdom from above. It is not being smart, or clever, or having the ability to win arguments. It is not being a Bible expert either, although knowing the Word of God is necessary and important for the Christian. It is God's supernatural endowment of *His wisdom* to the believer at a particular time, in a particular circumstance, to fulfill His purposes.

The word of wisdom is manifested frequently by Jesus in the Scriptures. The Pharisees asked Jesus, "Is it lawful to give tribute unto Caesar, or not?" (Matthew 22:17). This was a trick question. The taxation system of the Romans was unfair and burdensome for the common people. If Jesus said "pay the taxes," He would be perceived as condoning the oppression of Rome. If He said, "don't pay your taxes," He would have been fomenting rebellion against the authorities. His enemies thought they had him.

But he perceived their craftiness, and said unto them, Why tempt ye me?

Show me a penny (a denarius—a day's wage). Whose image and superscription hath it? They answered and said, Caesar's.

And he said unto them, Render therefore unto Caesar the things which be Caesar's, and unto God the things which be God's.

And they could not take hold of his words before the people: and they marvelled at his answer, and held their peace (Luke 20:23–26).

A word of wisdom, indeed!

In John chapter eight, Jesus manifested the word of wisdom when they brought the woman taken in adultery before him. He said "He that is without sin among you, let him first cast a stone at her" (John 8:7). Any one that cast a stone would be saying that God is a liar because the testimony of Scripture is that there is "none that doeth good" (Psalm 14:3), none without sin. The one casting the stone would himself be stoned by the others for calling God a liar. Therefore they all left, one by one.

God has given the word of wisdom to the church also. His people evidence the gift:

> *Stephen, full of faith and power, did great wonders and miracles among the people (Acts 6:8).*

> *And they (the enemies of the gospel) were not able to resist the wisdom and the spirit by which he spake (Acts 6:10).*

God has used the word of wisdom in my life.

One day at lunch, an acquaintance began to complain about TV evangelists and how dishonest he thought they were. Then he surprised me by attacking Billy Graham. He said he was "the worst one," and that "his organization had millions of dollars and would not use it to help the poor." I knew that was not true but did not know what to say. I had never heard anyone criticize Billy Graham before. I said "Bob, you are the first one I have ever heard say anything bad about Billy Graham." He looked at me convicted and stunned, said nothing else, and shortly left the table. There were several Christians sitting there who witnessed this, and they were blessed that God had silenced him and protected the name of His servant, Billy Graham. God, with a word of wisdom, pointed the searchlight of His Spirit into the soul of Bob, revealing his sinfulness and hypocrisy in speaking against the Lord's anointed. I later realized this was a word of wisdom God had given me to shut the mouth of His adversary. It is "Not by might, nor by power, but by my spirit, saith the LORD of hosts" (Zechariah 4:6).

Word of Knowledge

The word of knowledge is *logos gnoseos, gnosis* being the Greek for knowledge. We use this root word in medicine. Dia*gnosis* implies that we know what is wrong with the patient. As with the word of wisdom, the information is given supernaturally by the Holy Spirit. It is not natural knowledge. It is not being perceptive, or smart, or having a good memory. It has nothing to do with our innate abilities, or our IQ. It is God's supernatural endowment of *His knowledge* to the believer at a particular time, in a particular circumstance, to fulfill His purposes. Jesus manifested the word of knowledge in some powerful ways.

> *Jesus saw Nathaniel coming to him, and saith of him, Behold, an Israelite indeed, in whom is no guile!*

Nathaniel saith unto him, Whence knowest thou me? Jesus answered and said unto him, Before that Philip called thee, when thou wast under the fig tree, I saw thee (John 1:47–48).

Jesus saw Nathaniel, apparently in a vision, and knew, through word of knowledge, that he was "an Israelite indeed in whom is no guile." Jesus knew about him before he met him.

When Jesus talked with the Samaritan woman at the well, He told her:

Whosoever drinketh of the water that I shall give him shall never thirst; but the water that I shall give him shall be in him a well of water springing up into everlasting life.

The woman saith unto him, Sir, give me this water, that I thirst not, neither come hither to draw.

Jesus saith unto her, Go, call thy husband, and come hither.

The woman answered and said, I have no husband. Jesus said unto her, Thou hast well said, I have no husband:

For thou hast had five husbands; and he whom thou now hast is not thy husband: in that saidst thou truly.

*The woman saith unto him, Sir, I perceive that
thou art a prophet (John 4:14–19).*

Jesus knew all about this woman through
the word of knowledge from the Holy Spirit. He
knew exactly what to say to her to get her
attention, and touch her heart.

The word of wisdom and word of
knowledge are wonderful gifts for ministry.
They are especially valuable in counseling.
Sometimes it can take hours of talking to a
person before you really get to the root of their
problems. With the word of knowledge, God
can give it to you in an instant. With the word of
wisdom, God can also give you the solution to a
problem in a flash.

The Old Testament Prophet, Elisha, had a
very powerful gift of the word of knowledge.
The king of Syria made plans to attack the king
of Israel, but Elisha warned the king of Israel
and saved his life twice. The king of Syria got
upset and thought there was a spy among his
servants.

*He called his servants, and said unto them, Will
ye not show me which of us is for the king of
Israel? And one of his servants said, None, my
lord, O king: but Elisha, the prophet that is in*

> *Israel, telleth the king of Israel the words that*
> *thou speakest in thy bedchamber (2 Kings*
> *6:11–12).*

Elisha even knew what the king said in private to his wife.

Elisha was so tuned in to God that he was surprised when he did not know what was going on. There was a woman who was kind to Elisha, and she was rewarded by the birth of a son through the prophecy of Elisha. One day her son had a severe headache, and died. She got on a donkey and headed for Elisha. When she came to him in anguish and caught Elisha by the feet, his servant tried to push her away. Elisha told him to "Let her alone; for her soul is vexed within her: and the Lord hath hid it from me, and hath not told me" (2 Kings 4:27). Elisha was surprised when he did not have the word of knowledge. A prophet does not know everything, but only knows what the Lord chooses to reveal to him. The word of knowledge is a gift, a revelation from God.

When we lived in California, we had a good friend who was a very bright attorney. I witnessed to Bill on several occasions, but he would have nothing to do with Jesus Christ. He would argue with me about the reliability and authenticity of the Bible.

Bill had a good mind, but it got in the way of his accepting Christ. However, he always respected Gale and me for our faith in the Lord.

After we left California, one day we got a disturbing telephone call: Bill had a heart attack and was in the hospital. My wife, Gale said to me: "Bill is going to die. I want you to get on an airplane to California and go witness to him one last time." I went the next day. Bill looked fine. He did not even appear to be ill. He told me how glad he was to see me, and was touched that I had come all the way from Georgia because of his illness. I told him that we really loved him, and that Gale said I should come. I expressed our concern about his heart attack and said, "Bill, you look fine now, but God has given you a warning and another chance." For the first time, he listened intently as I told him about Jesus Christ and how much He loved him and had died for him. There were no arguments, no rebuttals. He was totally prepared to hear the gospel. The Lord opened Bill's heart that day and he asked Jesus to come into his life and save him.

We had prayer and Christian fellowship together for the first time. Bill thanked me for coming and for telling him about Jesus.

When I arrived home in Georgia, I shared with my wife the wonderful news of Bill's salvation. I said, "you were exactly right, honey, I was supposed to go to California to bring the Lord's salvation to Bill. However, his heart is doing fine, and the doctors say he will be okay." A few days later we received another telephone call. The night before, Bill had another heart attack. This one was much worse. They rushed him into cardiac surgery to try to save his life. Bill died on the operating table. He is with the Lord now.

My wife's earlier statements to me were word of knowledge ("Bill is going to die") and word of wisdom ("Go witness to him one last time").

How We Receive Revelation Information From God

I will pour out of my Spirit upon all flesh: and your sons and your daughters shall prophesy, and your young men shall see visions, and your old men shall dream dreams (Acts 2:17).

After we receive the gift of the word of knowledge or the word of wisdom, how do we actually receive the information from God? We may receive "the word" in several different ways:

1. Visions. Jesus told Nathaniel that he "saw" him under the tree. Peter received information from God in a vision at Simon the Tanner's house at Joppa. Many visions are found throughout Scripture.

2. Dreams. God gave Nebuchadnezzar and Daniel dreams representing world history. Pharaoh had dreams from God which were interpreted by Joseph.

3. The voice of the Lord. The Lord passed by and Elijah experienced a strong wind ripping up the mountains and the rocks, but the Lord was not in the wind. Then there was an earthquake, but the Lord was not in the earthquake. Next there was a fire, but the Lord was not in the fire. And "after the fire a still small voice" (1 Kings 19:12). "There came a voice unto him, and said, What doest thou here, Elijah?" (1 Kings 19:13). The Lord may speak to us directly. "And thine ears shall hear a word behind

thee, saying, This is the way, walk ye in it" (Isaiah 30:21). God spoke to Moses, "face to face."

4. A glimpse into the realm of the Spirit. Elisha and his servant were surrounded by a great host of the Syrian army in the city of Dothan. His servant was on the verge of panic. Elisha said, "Fear not: for they that be with us are more than they that be with them. And Elisha prayed and said, Lord, I pray thee, open his eyes that he may see. And the Lord opened the eyes of the young man; and he saw: and behold, the mountain was full of horses and chariots of fire round about Elisha" (2 Kings 6:16–17). This was neither a vision nor a dream. His servant got a glimpse into the supernatural realm, and saw the forces of God.

5. An impression from God. When the Apostle Paul was at Lystra, there was a crippled man who heard Paul speak. Paul, "steadfastly beholding him, and perceiving that he had faith to be healed, Said with a loud voice, Stand upright on thy feet. And he leaped and walked" (Acts 14:9–10).

Paul's perception came from the Lord, a word of knowledge.

6. Circumstances. Sometimes the things that happen bear the fingerprints of God. Even the unbelieving magicians of Pharaoh, when they could not create lice from the dust, as Moses and Aaron had done, "said unto Pharaoh, This is the finger (the hand) of God" (Exodus 8:19). God often speaks to us and guides us through the circumstances in our lives. "The steps of a good man are ordered by the Lord" (Psalm 37:23).

7. He speaks to us through others. Ananias laid his hands on Paul and said, "Brother Saul, the Lord, even Jesus, that appeared unto thee in the way as thou camest, hath sent me, that thou mightest receive thy sight, and be filled with the Holy Ghost" (Acts 9:17b).

God spoke to the prophet Balaam through a donkey in Numbers chapter twenty-two.

Discerning of Spirits

The third revelation gift is the discerning of Spirits. With this gift the Holy Spirit enables us to discern what is from God and what is from

Satan, and what is from the heart of man. This gift helps protect the body of Christ. I remember several years ago when I was attending Calvary Chapel, Costa Mesa, that I began reading books by a false teacher. Many others at Calvary were being deceived by him. One day Pastor Chuck Smith stood up in the pulpit and mentioned this man by name and said that he was a false teacher. I was shocked. At first I thought Pastor Chuck was a little narrow-minded. But I loved Pastor Chuck and his teaching and decided to wait and see what would happen. I prayed about it. Sure enough, the Lord revealed how dangerous this man's doctrines were. His teachings sterilized the ministry of a young evangelist who had led many to Christ. Pastor Chuck has the gift of discerning of Spirits.

This gift can be a painful one. I have since received the gift myself. It is difficult when you encounter a false teacher and many of your Christian friends are raving about how wonderful he is, and what a great teacher he is, and you know he is false. You tell your friends, and they do not believe you. I have had Christian "friends" that finally did not want to be around me anymore because they knew what I thought about their favorite teacher.

The gift is also necessary to determine if someone is demon possessed or not. Jesus of course had the gift, and cast out demons on many occasions.

Sometimes even God's people can be used by Satan. Discerning this can be difficult, because we do not expect it. Immediately after Peter said to Jesus, "Thou art the Christ, the Son of the living God" (Matthew 16:16), he tried to convince Jesus not to go to the cross. Jesus then said unto Peter, "Get thee behind me, Satan: thou art an offence unto me: for thou savourest not the things that be of God, but those that be of men" (Matthew 16:23). Peter was not demon possessed, but was the unwitting tool of the devil, the mouthpiece for Satan. He was under satanic influence.

Uses of the Revelation Gifts

The word of wisdom, word of knowledge, and discernment of spirits are each "revelation" gifts. Information is received supernaturally from God that we could not know in any other way. God may give us the information for various purposes. We may be called to pray for a need and not reveal it to anyone. We may be called to talk to someone to counsel them or try to help someone else. We may be called to warn others, as in the case of a false teacher. We may be called to use another gift along with a revelation. If we discern that someone is demon possessed, God might call us to use the gift of faith to cast out the demon.

The Revelation Gifts, When Spoken, Become Prophecy

When God calls us to speak forth the information He has revealed to us, it becomes prophecy. Prophecy is God speaking to people through a person, one of His vessels, with the gift of prophecy. He must reveal something to that person in order to speak. He reveals information through the revelation gifts. The revelation may be through word of knowledge, word of wisdom, or discerning of spirits, but when it is spoken forth, it becomes prophecy. In 1 Corinthians 14:26, there is no mention of prophecy, but there is mention of "revelations." The revelations mentioned in verse 26 are spoken forth as prophecy. In the context, in the next few verses, Paul instructs the church in judging prophecy, which is the same as instructing them in judging the revelations that were spoken. Remember my wife's word of

wisdom and word of knowledge about Bill and
his heart attack? She spoke these words to me:
"Bill is going to die . . . go witness to him . . . ."
This was a prophecy from the Lord.

When the information is given to the body
of Christ through a prophecy in a meeting, then
the prophecy must be judged in accordance with
1 Corinthians 14:29. This will be covered in the
section on prophecy.

The Power Gifts

The three power gifts are the gift of faith, the
working of miracles, and the gifts of healings.

The Gift of Faith

The gift of faith is not the same as saving
faith. With the gift of faith, God empowers the
believer to perform mighty acts of faith. The
prophet Elijah had a contest with the prophets
of Baal. They each set up an altar with an animal
sacrifice on it. The prophets of Baal prayed for
their god to consume their sacrifice. Nothing
happened. Then Elijah prayed at his altar to
God, and;

> *Then the fire of the Lord fell, and consumed the*
> *burnt sacrifice, and the wood, and the stones, and*
> *the dust, and licked up the water that was in the*

trench. And when all the people saw it, they fell on their faces: and they said, The Lord, he is the God; the Lord, he is the God (1 Kings 18:38–39).

Jesus promised us this kind of faith.

And Jesus answering saith unto them, Have faith in God. For verily I say unto you, That whosoever shall say unto this mountain, Be thou removed, and be thou cast into the sea; and shall not doubt in his heart, but shall believe that those things which he saith shall come to pass; he shall have whatsoever he saith (Mark 11:22–23).

Several years ago when I was at Calvary Chapel of Costa Mesa and conducting "Believer's Meetings," I received a telephone call late one night. Jack, one of the leaders at our meetings, called and said he thought his sister-in-law was demon-possessed. He shared with me how her father had died; she was not getting along with her mother, and in desperation, had gone to a seance to try to contact her dead father. She was not saved, and had made contact with a demon who had deceived her into thinking he was her father. He entered her and she became possessed. The family immediately noticed a change in her speech and behavior. When Jack found out about the seance, he realized what had happened. He called me at

1:00 A.M. and asked me to help. They lived an hour's drive away, so they were to arrive around 2:00 A.M. I awoke my wife, told her what was happening, and asked her to pray. I also said, "Why do these things always happen late at night when I am on call and have to work the next day?" I lay down to sleep for a while and the Lord spoke to my heart, "It will be done within an hour."

Jack and his family arrived at precisely 2:00 A.M. He was accompanied by his wife, his sister-in-law, and his mother-in-law. As I talked with his sister-in-law, she was fearful and spoke in strange voices at times. When I looked in her eyes, I saw only darkness. I talked with her, and periodically the demon would speak threatening things through her. I commanded him in the name of Jesus Christ to be silent. "I" did not rebuke him. I asked the Lord to rebuke him, as Michael the Archangel did with Satan when contending with him about the body of Moses (Jude 9).

It is important to remember that we do not rebuke demons. We ask the Lord to rebuke them. I also want to emphasize something else: at no time during this encounter did I feel fear. I felt absolute confidence that the Lord was in control, that He had authority over this demon, and that He was going to cast him out. I knew this demon had no power over any of us. I told her that if she wanted to be free, that Jesus Christ could set her free, but that she must accept Christ as her Savior if we cast the demon out. Otherwise the demon would return with others and re-inhabit her. She said she wanted to be free. We prayed for her and nothing seemed to happen. We prayed several more times, and she still was not delivered. We then prayed for God to show us what was wrong. He did. She was still very angry at her mother. Her mother then tenderly held her, prayed for her, wept, and asked her forgiveness. Suddenly, the demon was gone, light flooded her soul, she smiled, wept tears of joy, and embraced her mother. I talked to her some more about Jesus Christ, and she opened up her heart and received Him as her Savior. It was glorious.

When I went to bed, my wife asked me what time it was. I looked at my watch. It was 3:00 A.M. The Lord said it would be done within an hour—it was.

Another important point to remember is that we do not go demon chasing. I have encountered other people that I discerned were demon possessed, but felt no call of God to try to cast out the demon. We must remember the teaching of Scripture:

> *When the unclean spirit is gone out of a man, he walketh through dry places, seeking rest; and finding none, he saith, I will return unto my house whence I came out.*
>
> *And when he cometh, he findeth it swept and garnished. Then goeth he, and taketh to him seven other spirits more wicked than himself; and they enter in, and dwell there: and the last state of that man is worse than the first (Luke 11:24–26).*

This portion of Scripture is telling us that if a demon is cast out and is not replaced by the indwelling Spirit of God, the demon will return and bring others to repossess that person and they will be worse off than before the demon was cast out. It is very important to make sure that God has called you to cast out the demon, and that the person is ready to get saved. Though they may be possessed, the demon does not have absolute control, otherwise they would not have the will to come to Jesus for deliverance. The demon would like to keep them as far from Jesus as he can. When they come to Jesus for deliverance, He says He accepts them. They are accepted in the beloved.

The gift of faith is needed to cast out demons. But notice what I said above. Faith is not something I worked up in order to cast out the demon. It was absolute trust, absolute confidence in *God's ability* to cast out the demon. If it was up to me to work up the faith, I would have been filled with fear. At no time did I put my faith in my faith, or my abilities, but it was in the power of God, and God alone.

The Working of Miracles

The gift of the working of miracles is literally in Greek, "the operation of powers." It is the operation of the power of God with the Holy Spirit working in the life of a believer. God has created certain natural laws by which He runs the universe. A miracle is the temporary suspension by God of one of these laws.

We are all familiar with the law of gravity. This law was suspended when Jesus came to his disciples on the sea of Galilee, walking on the water. It was also suspended when Peter walked on the water toward Jesus. When Peter's faith failed because of fear, the suspension of the law was no longer in effect, and he began to sink. Jesus caught his hand and saved him. Walking on water is a miracle.

The first law of thermodynamics states that matter is neither being created nor destroyed. This law was suspended when Jesus performed the miracle of the five loaves and two fishes in which he fed five thousand men.

Finally, at the wedding at Cana, Jesus turned water into wine. One substance does not naturally change into another substance. Mere water became wine in this miracle. It also became the best wine.

God also uses His people with this gift.

God wrought special miracles by the hands of Paul: So that from his body were brought unto the sick handkerchiefs or aprons, and the diseases departed from them, and the evil spirits went out of them (Acts 19:11–12).

Gifts of Healings

We commonly call this gift, the gift of healing. Both words are plural in the original Greek. It is literally, "gifts of healings." This implies there are different kinds of gifts, and different kinds of healings that take place with the use of this gift. God created man spirit, soul, and body. When Adam and Eve sinned in Eden, their spirits died that day. Thus all mankind has come from Adam and is made up of living souls inhabiting living bodies, but with dead spirits. We need healing at times in all these realms. The unsaved natural man needs spiritual healing, just as the one who is demon possessed does. When we are born again, our spirits come alive in Christ. Salvation is the greatest healing of all. Because of the sin principle in us, and sin acts which we commit, our souls and bodies become ill. Sometimes we need emotional healing of the soul. Sometimes we need physical healing of the body. Jesus healed in all these areas.

Jesus healed spiritually when he cast seven demons out of Mary Magdalene. He healed physically when he healed the blind, and when he healed lepers. Matthew chapter four mentions healings by Jesus in all these areas.

> *They brought unto him all sick people that were taken with divers (diverse) diseases and torments, and those which were possessed with devils, and those which were lunatick, and those that had the palsy; and he healed them (Matthew 4:24).*

Those that were demon-possessed were healed spiritually. The lunatics were insane and were healed emotionally, in their souls, and possibly healed physically in the case of chemical imbalance causing insanity. Those with the palsy were paralyzed, and were healed physically.

The apostles, especially Peter and Paul, healed in these areas also. God used Peter and John to heal the lame man at the gate of the temple called Beautiful. God used Paul to heal the cripple man at Lystra. These are only two of many examples. God has given to the church the gifts of healings. Different people receive different manifestations of the gift for different kinds of healings in the body of Christ. Pastor Chuck has often said, the gift of healing sometimes may be a gift from God bestowed directly on the sick person that he might be healed.

Charismatic Gifts in Romans Twelve

Other gifts of the Spirit are mentioned in Romans chapter twelve.

> *Having then gifts differing according to the grace that is given to us, whether **prophecy**, let us prophesy according to the proportion of faith;*

*Or **ministry,** let us wait on our ministering: or he that teacheth, on **teaching;***

*Or he that exhorteth, on **exhortation:** he that **giveth,** let him do it with simplicity; he that **ruleth,** with diligence; he that showeth **mercy,** with cheerfulness (Romans 12:6–8, emphasis added).*

Wayne Taylor, in his excellent book, *Practical Christian Living,*[1] in the Calvary Basics Series, elaborates on the use of these gifts. He states, "these are what pastor Jon Courson calls the 'Motivational Gifts of the Holy Spirit.' Which of these gifts you have will determine how you are motivated in serving the Lord."

He continues with a humorous illustration:

"Let's suppose I'm preaching on a Sunday morning and Robert, one of my assistant pastors, decides to get me a glass of water. But as Robert is coming down the aisle with the glass of water, he trips, breaks the glass, and water goes everywhere. How would you respond to Robert? If you were a prophet, you would proclaim truth saying, 'Robert, my son.

---

[1]. *Practical Christian Living,* by Wayne Taylor (Santa Ana, CA: The Word For Today Publishers), 1995.

Be careful how thy walkest, for there are many stumbling blocks sayeth the Lord.' If your gift was service, you would say, 'Let's get a broom and mop,' and you'd pitch in to clean the mess up. But if your gift was teaching, you'd say, 'Robert, when you're walking down the aisle, you've got to lift your feet a certain distance from the ground, because that rug has fiber that is very blunt. And *blunt* in the Greek is the word "stumbeleko."' If your gift was exhortation, you would say, 'Robert, you klutz! You know better than that. Get up! Walk straight next time!' If your gift was giving, you'd say, 'Let me replace that broken glass, and if you hurt your ankle, I'll pay the doctor's bill.' If your gift was leading, you'd say, 'Wayne, come here. Help me pick up Robert. Kim, go get a broom. Cathy, get a mop.' If your gift was mercy, you'd say, 'Oh Robert, my dear. Are you all right? You must feel terrible. Come here and cry on my shoulder.'"

Gifts of Men for the Church

Ephesians 4:8 says, "he ascended up on high . . . and gave gifts unto men." Paul later described these gifts: "And he gave some, apostles; and some, prophets; and some, evangelists; and some, pastors, and teachers" (Ephesians 4:11). The purpose of these gifts is:

> *For the perfecting of the saints, for the work of the ministry, for the edifying of the body of Christ: Till we all come in the unity of the faith, and of the knowledge of the Son of God, unto a perfect man, unto the measure of the stature of the fulness of Christ (Ephesians 4:12–13).*

The Greek word for *gifts* here is *"doma,"* not *"charisma,"* as used in 1 Corinthians 12:4. Scofield states, "In Corinthians the gifts *(charisma)* are *spiritual enablements* for specific service; in Ephesians the gifts *(doma)* are *men* who have such enablements."[1] Paul, in 1 Corinthians 12:28, speaks of both sets of gifts. Gifts of men are the apostles, prophets, and teachers. Spiritual enablements are miracles, healings, helps, governments, and tongues.

Teaching Is More Important Than Miracles

The order in 1 Corinthians 12:28 is interesting.

---

[1]. The Scofield Study Bible, edited by C.I. Scofield (New York: Oxford University Press). Emphasis mine.

> *And God hath set some in the church, first*
> *apostles, secondarily prophets, thirdly teachers,*
> *after that miracles, then gifts of healings, helps,*
> *governments, diversities of tongues.*

No one would argue that the apostles and the prophets are pre-eminent in the church. But note that the ministry of teaching is more important than the working of miracles or the gifts of healings. I do not think most of the body of Christ believes this today. If an anointed teacher of the Bible came to our town at the same time as someone with the working of miracles, which service do you think most of the Christians would attend? Most Christians underestimate the value of good, solid, anointed expository teaching of the Word of God. This is the "secret of success" of the Calvary Chapel ministries. Nearly thirty years ago, God called an anointed teacher, Pastor Chuck Smith, to teach other men to teach His Word.

The balanced teaching of God's Word; flexible obedience to God's Word; the power of the baptism of the Holy Spirit; the scriptural use of the gifts of the Spirit; and anointed worship and praise have made the Calvary Chapel ministries what they are today. The foundation of all this is the ministry of the teaching of the

Word of God. I have watched "miracle ministries" come and go. I have seen the hype of "healing ministries" fade with the passing of the healer. "But the Word of the Lord endureth forever" (1 Peter 1:25). I am not denying the validity of those ministries, but the ministry of the teaching of the Word is elevated above them by the Scriptures. The Word is elevated above the name of God in Scripture. "Thou hast magnified thy word above all thy name" (Psalm 38:2). We cannot overemphasize the importance of the teaching of God's Word.

Operation of the Gifts

Many traditional Pentecostals criticize us at Calvary Chapel. I have heard people make statements like, "I don't see the gifts being used here." What they mean is, they do not see the use of tongues in the general services. But the gifts are in operation. One of the greatest gifts that God has blessed us with at Calvary Chapel is the gift of teaching. He has raised up some tremendous Bible teachers in the various Calvary Chapels. I see the body ministry in operation everywhere at Calvary Chapel, Tallahassee, and Calvary Chapel, Thomasville. I frequently see people before and after church praying for one another, manifesting the gift of mercy. I hear those with the gift of exhortation encouraging one another. I have seen God give Pastor Kent Nottingham the word of knowledge while teaching and preaching. I have heard beautiful words of prophecy come from the lips of Pastor Chuck when he dismisses the people at Calvary Chapel, Costa Mesa. Yes, the gifts are in use in the Calvary Chapels. They are used in a manner which glorifies the Lord. They are not used to glorify God's vessels.

The Body of Christ

For by one Spirit are we all baptized into one body, whether we be Jews or Gentiles, whether we be bond or free; and have been all made to drink into one Spirit (1 Corinthians 12:13).

When we are born again, we are baptized into the body of Christ *by* the Holy Spirit. This is salvation. This is different from the baptism *with* the Holy Spirit, mentioned by Jesus in Acts 1:5, which is for empowerment to be His witnesses. When you are baptized *by* the Spirit into the body of Christ, then *you have the Spirit*. When you are baptized *with* the Holy Spirit, then *the Spirit has you*.

Thus the baptism with the Holy Spirit is a _separate experience_ from salvation. When we are saved, the Holy Spirit comes to live inside us. When we are baptized with the Holy Spirit, the Holy Spirit comes upon us, anointing us, empowering us for the work of God.

Objections to the Baptism of the Holy Spirit

Many denominations do not believe in a separate experience of the baptism with (or of) the Holy Spirit. There are two basic positions that these denominations take:

1. Some teach that when you are saved, you also receive the baptism of the Holy Spirit at the same time. They believe that the Scripture, "by one Spirit are we all baptized into one body" (1 Corinthians 12:13), refers to a single experience of salvation combined with a baptism of the Holy Spirit into the body of Christ. They also teach that "One Lord, one faith, _one baptism_" (Ephesians 4:5) excludes a "second blessing" of the baptism with the Holy Spirit. They teach that since there is only "one baptism," when you get saved, you get it all, including the baptism of the Holy Spirit.

One problem with this teaching is that there are several baptisms mentioned in Scripture. There is water baptism (Acts 8:36). There is the baptism of John (Acts 18:25), the baptism of repentance (Mark 1:4), the baptism of regeneration (1 Peter 3:21), the baptism into the death of Christ (Romans 6:3), and the baptism unto Moses (1 Corinthians 10:2). And there is the baptism of the Holy Spirit (Acts 11:16).

The preceding verse in Ephesians explains what the Apostle Paul means by "one baptism." "There is *one body*, and one Spirit, even as ye are called in one hope of your calling"; (Ephesians 4:4) "One Lord, one faith, *one baptism*" (Ephesians 4:5) The "one baptism" speaks of being baptized into "one body" (1 Corinthians 12:13), the body of Christ. This refers to the unity of the body of Christ, not a baptism which excludes the existence of other types of baptisms referred to in Scripture. As mentioned previously, baptism *by* the Holy Spirit is not the same as baptism *with* the Holy Spirit. Salvation is different from the empowerment of the Spirit. This is demonstrated on several occasions in the book of Acts.

Those who hold to this theology believe the gifts are no longer in operation today. It is interesting that they believe they have the power of the Holy Spirit, but show little evidence of it as demonstrated in the book of Acts.

2. Some teach that the baptism of the Holy Spirit is not for today. They believe it was given at Pentecost to establish the church. Then it was given by the apostles to the early believers with the laying on of hands. However, when the last of the apostles died, the baptism of the Holy Spirit was no longer given. Since the canon of Scripture was complete by then, the baptism was no longer needed. The same logic applies to the gifts of the Spirit. Some theologians use 1 Corinthians chapter thirteen to try to prove this point.

> *Charity (love) never faileth: but whether (where) there be prophecies, they shall fail (no longer be in operation): whether (where) there be tongues, they shall cease; whether (where) there be knowledge, it shall vanish away.*
>
> *For we know in part, and we prophesy in part.*
>
> *But when that which is perfect is come, then that which is in part shall be done away (1 Corinthians 13:8–10).*

When That Which Is Perfect Is Come

The time honored interpretation of verse 10 has been, "that which is perfect is come" refers to Jesus Christ and His Second Coming. At that time, we will receive our new bodies.

> *Beloved, now are we the sons of God, and it doth not yet appear what we shall be: but we know that, when he shall appear, we shall be like him; for we shall see him as he is (1 John 3:2).*

When we are like Him, we will have the same attributes that He has, except that He is God. We will no longer need the gifts of the Holy Spirit. Therefore, prophecies, tongues, and word of knowledge, will cease to be in operation.

A New Interpretation

In the early 1900's a new interpretation of 1 Corinthians 13:10 was put forth by certain fundamentalists. The new teaching states, "that which is perfect is come," is not Christ, but the Bible. Those who ascribe to this theology believe the gifts of the Holy Spirit were imparted only through the apostles, and when the last of the apostles died, the gifts passed out of existence. They were no longer needed anyway, since the completion of the canon of Scripture gave us the full revelation of the Word of God, the Bible. Therefore, the gifts of the Holy Spirit were only temporary and are not for today.

There are several major problems with this interpretation of Scripture.

A. The gift of prophecy will continue until the time of the end. In Acts 2:17–21, Peter gives the scriptural basis for the baptism with the Holy Spirit at Pentecost. He quotes Joel 2:28–32. The prophecy of Joel starts with God pouring out His Spirit upon all flesh, continues through the Great Tribulation, and ends with the Second Coming of Jesus Christ. During this time, from Pentecost to the Second Coming, sons, daughters, servants, and handmaidens will be exercising the *gift of prophecy.* There is no mention in Scripture that this gift would cease after the death of the apostles. Further, the two witnesses in Revelation chapter eleven, will prophesy during the Great Tribulation. The gift of prophecy will continue until the Second Coming of Christ.

B. If we believe the gifts are not for today, then the Holy Spirit wasted a lot of Scripture instructing us in something that passed out of use as soon as the canon was complete. How frustrating for the church throughout the ages, to read about healings, miracles, great works of faith, and comforting prophecies, and then God slams the book closed and says: "I'm sorry, that is not for you, all the apostles are dead."

C. The next two verses:

When I was a child, I spake as a child, I understood as a child, I thought as a child: but when I became a man, I put away childish things (1 Corinthians 13:11).

In the context, with the new interpretation, the gifts of the Holy Spirit would be the "childish things" which would be put away. I have read Bible commentaries which, to my dismay, called the gifts, especially tongues, "childish things." Certainly the gifts have been misused and seemed childish, especially the use of tongues at times, but what about the apostle's use of the gifts of the Spirit? Is Paul calling that childish? Paul said, "I thank my God I speak with tongues more than ye all" (1 Corinthians 14:18). Was the healing of the lame man at the gate of the temple which is called Beautiful in Acts 3, a "childish thing?" When Peter went to the house of Cornelius in Acts 10, and the gift of the Holy Spirit was poured out upon them and they spoke with tongues and magnified God, was that a "childish thing?" Was the prophesying of the four virgin daughters of Philip the evangelist in Acts 21, a "childish thing?" I think not. The book of Acts is filled with examples of childish things if that is the theological position one takes in regard to the gifts of the Holy Spirit.

What are the "childish things" that Paul refers to then? In the context, it is the carnal use of the gifts of the Holy Spirit, the operation of the gifts without love. People are especially prone to misuse tongues and prophecy in this way. The Apostle spends the whole next chapter instructing the believers in their proper use, so that they may put away childish things. "When I became a man, I put away childish things" (1 Corinthians 13:11). Becoming a man is to mature in Jesus Christ, to grow up in Him, to grow in His love and grace, to leave the old carnal life, and to live for Christ, and Christ alone. Putting away "childish things" is casting aside carnality, leaving the old life of the flesh, and ministering through the power of the Holy Spirit in love. Love is not a substitute for the gifts, but the *agape* love of God is the driving force for the gifts.

> For **now** we see through a glass, darkly; but **then** face to face: **now** I know in part; but **then** shall I know even as also I am known (1 Corinthians 13:12).

In the traditional interpretation of verse 10, "that which is perfect is come" is Jesus Christ at His Second Coming. Therefore, the "now" in verse 12 lasts from the day of Paul up to the time of the Second Coming. So the "now" for us today is the present time. We are living in the "now." "Then" is still future. Read verse 12 again. We presently do not see things clearly, we see through a glass darkly, like a smoked glass. When Christ comes, "then" we will see Him face to face. Now we know in part; we do not yet have the full revelation of God. But when Christ comes, "then" He will reveal all things to us.

The new interpretation of verse 10 is, "that which is perfect is come" is the Bible, not Christ. This implies that the "now" is past, and we are living in the "then." The "now" was Paul's day, the time of the apostles. "Then" is today. Paul, and those of his day, saw through a glass darkly, because they did not yet have the full revelation of God, the complete canon of Scripture. Today we have the complete canon, the Bible, and therefore no longer see through a glass darkly, but can now have a full understanding of the things of God through His Word. We now know, even as we are known. This is the culmination of the logic of that interpretation.

Do we really believe this? Do we have a full understanding, a full revelation of God? Certainly the New Testament Scriptures have wonderfully broadened our understanding of God through His Son. But can we now say that we see "face to face?" Paul said *he* saw "through a glass, darkly." Do we have greater clarity of vision into the things of God than the Apostle Paul? I do not. I believe, "eye hath not seen, nor ear heard, neither have entered into the heart of man, the things which God hath prepared for them that love him" (1 Corinthians 2:9).

We are still waiting for "that which is perfect" to come, Jesus Christ. Then we will see "face to face." Then the gifts of the Holy Spirit, that which is in part, shall be done away (1 Corinthian 13:10). So the gifts did not cease with the completion of the canon of Scripture. They will cease with the Second Coming of Christ.

The Bible is perfect. But we are not waiting for the written Word, we are waiting for the Living Word. We shall behold *Him!*

D. Finally, what about the millions of believers who exercise the gifts of the spirit today. They are empowered by the Holy Spirit to minister to the body of Christ with these gifts. How is it that I have a friend who speaks beautiful French in tongues, and another who speaks Greek in his prayer language. Neither understand nor ever studied these languages, but they speak them fluently when praying.

I must add that there is some foolishness going around today in the body of Christ masquerading as gifts of the Spirit. Being "slain in the Spirit" is not a gift of the Spirit, and is not a biblical experience. "Holy laughter" is not a gift of the Spirit and also is not biblical. Barking like dogs, or roaring like lions in a church service did not occur in the Bible. Unscriptural practices such as these only serve to confuse Christians and those outside the church as to what the gifts of the Spirit really are. Again, the remedy is the Word of God, the Bible. What saith the Scriptures?

In summary, one group objects to a "second blessing" of the baptism of the Holy Spirit because they think they received it when they were saved. Another group objects because they think God no longer bestows the baptism today.

Both of these positions are taught by some good Christian theologians, but both rob the believer of the power of the baptism of the Holy Spirit. To say you have something you do not, does not give it to you—it prevents you from asking for it. To say that God no longer empowers the church with the power of the baptism of the Holy Spirit, but that the Bible alone is enough for us, also strips the church of the power of the Spirit. I am amazed that so many otherwise excellent Bible teachers are blind in this area. They teach against the power of God with such tenacity. I do not know why. In the mainstream denominations such as the Assemblies of God, and other traditional Pentecostal Denominations, there are millions of loving, dedicated, Spirit-filled Christians who speak in tongues, prophesy, and exercise other wonderful gifts of the Spirit. Where is this power coming from? Are these teachers willing to write off "so great a cloud of witnesses"

(Hebrews 12:1), as not being empowered by God, but from some other source?

I think spiritual pride is what blinds most of these teachers. When you have spent much of your life teaching against something, reversing your stand, humbling yourself, and saying, "I was wrong," is very difficult. Eyes like this can only be opened by prayer and the power of the Spirit.

I frequently encounter Christians who love the Lord but have been taught against the baptism of the Holy Spirit and the gifts. When told they can experience these blessings today, they get very concerned. They want to make sure they are obeying God and Scripture. I show them the Scriptures promising the baptism and the gifts, and ask them to search for themselves to see if they can find anything in the Bible which says the baptism of the Holy Spirit is not for today, or the gifts are no longer in use. I remind them that Jesus said,

> *If ye then, being evil, know how to give good gifts unto your children: how much more shall your Heavenly Father give the Holy Spirit to them that ask him? (Luke 11:13).*

I do it in love. I do not argue about it. I also challenge them to just ask God to give them everything He has for them, and to be open to receive from Him. I have seen many of them receive after reading the Scriptures and seeking God's will in prayer.

The Spoken Gifts

Since much of the activity at an Afterglow Service consists of the use of the spoken gifts, we will take a close look at God's instructions for the use of those gifts in 1 Corinthians chapter fourteen. The Apostle Paul listed many gifts of the Spirit in 1 Corinthians chapter twelve. Then he told us in chapter thirteen that we should exercise those gifts in love.

A More Excellent Way

Paul says, "I will show you a more excellent way:" the way of *agape*, the way of love (1 Corinthians 12:31). Another translation is "I will show you the most excellent way." He is not suggesting that love is a substitute for the gifts, but that love should be the motivating force for their use.

> *Beloved, let us love one another: for love is of God; and every one that loveth is born of God,*

*and knoweth God. He that loveth not knoweth
not God, for God is love (1 John 4:7–8).*

Love for others, and love for Christ is to be
the pre-eminent motivation.

*Though I speak with the tongues of men and of
angels, and have not charity (love), I am become
as sounding brass, or a tinkling cymbal. And
though I have the gift of prophecy, and
understand all mysteries, and all knowledge; and
though I have all faith, so that I could remove
mountains, and have not charity (love), I am
nothing (1 Corinthians 13:1–2).*

The gifts without love are worthless. Love
without the gifts lacks power. The gifts of the
Holy Spirit, motivated by love, or love,
empowered by the gifts of the Spirit, are what
"turned the world upside down" in the book of
Acts.

The Spoken Gifts and Their Use in the Church

I find it interesting that we have nearly a
whole chapter in Scripture devoted to the
spoken gifts. We do not have a chapter telling us
how to operate the gift of healing, or the
working of miracles. There is no explanation of
how the word of wisdom or the word of
knowledge might come to us. But in 1

Corinthians fourteen, God gives us almost a whole chapter on the vocal gifts. Why? They are the gifts most commonly misused and abused, and we need very detailed instructions for their operation. I do not see anyone abusing the gift of healing in that too many people are being healed. I do not see too many miracles being performed. But I do see people abusing the gift of tongues, and prophecy. This was happening in the church at Corinth, and it is happening now. The abuse and misuse of the spoken gifts is prevalent in the church today.

Many churches today ignore the instructions in Scripture. They have developed certain traditions in the use of gifts. They use a certain voice, a certain tone, a certain volume. I once visited a charismatic denominational church. At one point in the service, the person who took me warned, "Now it's time for brother Jones (not his real name) to speak." Sure enough, brother Jones spoke, and everybody heard him. He spoke out loudly in his prayer language, and then gave a prophecy that he thought was the interpretation. He was the self-appointed tongues-speaker, and interpreter for each of their worship services. I met him later. He was a nice man, but he was locked in tradition. He would have been shocked if I had pointed out to him that he was not using tongues in accordance with Scripture. God's Word must be our standard and guide, and not the traditions of men.

Among the gifts, the use of the spoken gifts seems to cause the most confusion in the body of Christ, but all the problems are resolved by obeying Scripture.

Prophecy Is the Pre-eminent Spoken Gift

Follow after charity (love) and desire spiritual gifts, but rather (especially) that ye may prophesy (1 Corinthians 14:1).

The *agape* love of Jesus Christ is to be our motivation for the use of the gifts of the Spirit. Any other motivation is wrong. They are not for our power, to build big ministries, or to make others think we are super-spiritual. The gifts are given to us to minister to one another. We are to desire the gifts of the spirit. That is good, it is not selfish. Then he says we are to especially desire the gift of prophecy.

We Speak to God in Tongues

*For he that speaketh in an **unknown tongue** speaketh not unto men, but **unto God**: for no*

> *man understandeth him; howbeit in the spirit he*
> *speaketh mysteries (14:2, emphasis added).*

This Scripture, if obeyed, would change most charismatic churches overnight. A common error by those who speak in tongues is thinking they are giving others a "message in tongues." Paul says, when we speak in tongues, we are not speaking to one another, we are speaking to God. There is no such thing as a message to another person in tongues. Another person may overhear you speaking in tongues and understand what you are saying, but you are not speaking to him, but to God. This is what happened the day of Pentecost. The disciples were not speaking to the people from those seventeen different nations, they were speaking to God. As they spoke to God and praised Him for His wonderful works, the visitors in Jerusalem overheard what they were saying and were amazed. Similarly, when Peter went to the house of Cornelius and told them about Jesus, "the Holy Ghost fell on all them which heard the word" (Acts 10:44). "They heard them speak with tongues, and magnify God" (Acts 10:46). In each case, they were speaking to God, praising Him for His wonderful works, and magnifying Him.

No Message to the Church in Tongues

So the Scriptures do not speak of a message in tongues to the believers. Likewise, there is no such thing as a message in tongues to the church. When you speak in tongues, you are not speaking to individual people or to the church, you are speaking to God.

As we will see later in this chapter, when someone speaks in tongues in an assembly of believers, there must be an interpretation. The gift of interpretation of tongues is a sister gift to tongues. With this gift one is able to understand and speak forth what was said in tongues.

When someone speaks in tongues and another interprets, the interpretation is directed to God. Remember, "he that speaketh in an unknown tongue speaketh not unto men, but unto God" (1 Corinthians 14:2). The interpretation might be something like, "We love you and praise you, oh heavenly Father."

God Speaks to Us in Prophecy

But he that prophesieth speaketh unto men to edification, and exhortation, and comfort (1 Corinthians 14:3, emphasis added).

Prophecy is from the Greek *"pro"* (forth) *"phemi"* (to speak), meaning to speak forth for another (God). With the gift of prophecy, the Holy Spirit speaks through one person to others. Prophecy is God speaking to us. So words of encouragement might come forth in a prophecy like, "I love you my children, I am with you, I will never leave you nor forsake you."

An Interpretation of Tongues or a Prophecy?

In the prophecy above, God is speaking, so it is not an interpretation of what someone said in tongues. Why then is there confusion about this in many churches?

When the gifts are in operation, we often see tongues and prophecy in use simultaneously. Because some believers do not realize that an interpretation is directed to God, they often give a prophecy after someone speaks in tongues, thinking they are giving the interpretation. When church leaders do it wrong, the flock tends to follow the leader, and then unscriptural traditions develop in which a prophecy is substituted for the interpretation of tongues. Traditions are hard to change.

But remember, with an interpretation of tongues, men speak to God, whereas in prophecy, God speaks to men. *Tongues* go up *to God from men, prophecy* comes down *from God to men.* If we will just remember that simple concept, we will not get confused about what constitutes an interpretation of tongues.

Recently after a Believer's Meeting at Calvary Chapel, Tallahassee, a man came up to me after the service. He was visiting, and came from a traditional Pentecostal denomination. He had noted that our interpretations of tongues were spoken to God. He said that in their services, "messages in tongues" were frequently given to them, and they were a tremendous blessing.

I showed him 1 Corinthians 14:2. He read it, but then said, "How could we be doing it wrong? We are getting so blessed." I told him the Bible is the final authority, not how blessed we feel. He still could not accept it, and went away unsatisfied, unconvinced. Tradition is hard to break. Obedience to this portion of Scripture is one of the major differences in the use of the gifts between Calvary Chapels and most Pentecostal and charismatic churches.

Obedience to Scripture Protects the Body of Christ

Someone once said to me, "Aren't you being a little nit-picky about all of this? Why does it matter whether I gave a prophecy or an interpretation of a tongue?"

First, it matters because Scripture makes a distinction between an interpretation of tongues and prophecy, and therefore, we should too.

Second, there is room for much mischief when it is not done according to the Word. For instance, suppose you spoke in tongues in the church and someone then announced, "Here's the interpretation: Next month there is going to be a great earthquake and our whole town will be destroyed." Since you did not know what you were saying when you spoke in tongues (1 Corinthians 14:2), how could you deny that is what you said? It would put you in a difficult situation. The "interpreter" would say, "That's what you said." But when we recognize that his "interpretation" was not spoken to God, but to men, we conclude it cannot be the true interpretation of your tongue. We are then able to say confidently to the interpreter, "That is not what was said in tongues."

Obedience to Scripture protects the body of Christ.

Since what he spoke was to the church, if it is from God, then it would be a prophecy. We must then judge whether it is truly a prophecy from God. We will cover this when we discuss the use of the gift of prophecy in the church later in this section.

The latter portion of 1 Corinthians 14:3 shows the beauty of what a prophecy from God will do for us. In modern English, it should build us up (edification), stir us up (exhortation), and cheer us up (comfort).

He that speaketh in an unknown tongue edifieth (builds up) himself; but he that prophesieth edifieth (builds up) the church (1 Corinthians 14:4).

When I speak in tongues, I build up myself in the faith. When I prophesy to the body of Christ, I build up the church, the believers.

I would that ye all spake with tongues, but rather (more so) that ye prophesied: for greater is he that prophesieth than he that speaketh with tongues, except he interpret, that the church may receive edifying (1 Corinthians 14:5).

It is Paul's desire that we all speak in tongues, but as we shall see later, primarily in our private prayer lives. When we are with other believers, the gift of prophecy is a better gift to exercise. A prophecy is given in our own language. With prophecy, God can speak to others through us, and no interpretation is required. When an interpretation of tongues is given, the church is edified, for the believers then understand what was spoken to God in tongues. However, prophecy is a better gift for us to minister to one another.

We Should Pray for the Gift of Interpretation

Wherefore let him that speaketh in an unknown tongue pray that he may interpret (1 Corinthians 14:13).

The understanding comes through the gift of interpretation. Those with the gift of tongues should pray for the sister gift of the interpretation of tongues.

My Spirit Prays in Tongues

For if I pray in an unknown tongue, my spirit prayeth, but my understanding is unfruitful (1 Corinthians 14:14).

When I pray in tongues my spirit prays. God the Holy Spirit, in communion with my spirit, gives me words to speak to God the Father, in a language I do not understand. This is an act of faith on my part. I must trust the Holy Spirit. I do not know what I am saying, but I know that it is the right prayer, because God himself is giving me the words to pray.

Paul Spoke in Tongues More Than All of Them

I thank my God, I speak with tongues more than ye all (1 Corinthians 14:18).

Here we have it from the lips of the Apostle Paul: he spoke in tongues, and he spoke in tongues that all of them. He was baptized with the Holy Spirit in Acts 9:17. We are not told when he received tongues, but from this Scripture, we know not only that he had the gift, but that he exercised it frequently.

Tongues Is Primarily for Our Private Prayer Life

Yet in the church I had rather speak five words with my understanding, that by my voice I might teach others also, than ten thousand words in an unknown tongue (1 Corinthians 14:19).

Paul's use of the gift of tongues was primarily in his private prayer life. As we will see in the next few verses, speaking in tongues in the assembly of believers is permitted only on a limited basis. But Paul spoke in tongues a lot, more than all of them. How? He spoke quietly to himself, and to God. That is what he means when he tells us to "Pray without ceasing" (1 Thessalonians 5:17). The only way we can do that is in our prayer language. I can be busy at work, and still be praying in tongues, in my prayer language.

> *Brethren, be not children in understanding: howbeit in malice be ye children, but in understanding be men (1 Corinthians 14:20).*

He is telling them to grow up, to mature spiritually in Christ in their use of the gifts, especially tongues. Many Christians misuse and abuse tongues. Some think having the gift makes them more spiritual than others, so they get puffed up with pride in their use of the gift. They often use the gift to draw attention to themselves, so that others in the body of Christ will think they are super-spiritual. This is a carnal use of tongues. It is possible to use the gifts in the flesh, without love, as Paul said in 1 Corinthians 13:1–2.

> *If therefore the whole church be come together into one place, and all speak with tongues, and there come in those that are unlearned, or unbelievers, will they not say that ye are mad (insane)? (1 Corinthians 14:23).*

If the whole church is speaking in tongues simultaneously, and there is no interpretation, believers who do not understand, and unbelievers who cannot understand, will think you are all crazy.

> *But if all prophesy, and there come in one that believeth not, or one unlearned, he is convinced of all, he is judged of all (1 Corinthians 14:24).*

Prophecy would be understood by the listeners. A believer who has not experienced the gifts, or an unbeliever, hearing prophecy from God, would be convicted by the Holy Spirit of his sins.

> *And thus are the secrets of his heart made manifest; and so falling down on his face he will worship God, and report that God is in you of a truth (1 Corinthians 14:25).*

The secrets of his heart are revealed, and he repents and worships God. He recognizes that God is speaking through the body of Christ to him, and that God is present in them. What a glorious gift! No wonder the Apostle Paul said that we should especially desire the gift of prophecy.

> *How is it then, brethren? when ye come together, every one of you hath a psalm, hath a doctrine, hath a tongue, hath a revelation, hath an interpretation. Let all things be done unto edifying (1 Corinthians 14:26).*

This is our key Scripture for a Believer's Meeting. These are the activities that are appropriate when the believers gather together: singing praises to God, teaching the Word, speaking in tongues (in a limited way), revelations from God given as prophecy, and the interpretation of tongues. What a tremendous meeting, when done decently and order, according to Scripture. What chaos when done in the flesh, without the interpretation of tongues, with multiple people speaking in tongues and prophesying whenever they feel like it, interrupting the teaching of the Word, and without regard to godly order. Therefore, God gives us very strict, narrow guidelines for the use of tongues and prophecy in a meeting.

Tongues in the Assembly Is Limited to Two or Three, and Must be Interpreted

If any man speak in an unknown tongue, let it be by two, or at the most by three, and that by course (in order); and let one (someone) interpret (1 Corinthians 14:27).

When there is speaking in tongues in a gathering of believers, there should be only two or three utterances in tongues, and no more. It should be done in an orderly manner, allowing two or three different people to speak, one after the other, and not simultaneously. After each one speaks in tongues, there should be an interpretation of that tongue before moving on to the next tongue, prophecy, or whatever else the Holy Spirit might have in mind for the meeting. There is no "official interpreter." Anyone with the gift of interpretation (who receives an interpretation from the Lord), could give the interpretation.

An interpretation is not a translation. People may receive interpretations from the Lord that differ somewhat from one another. When I first received the gift of interpretation, it bothered me that I did not get exactly the same words in my interpretations that others received when they gave the interpretation. I thought maybe I was not listening to God properly. Someone correctly pointed out to me that an interpretation is not a literal translation of what was said. It is an interpretation, filtered through the vessel that is speaking. God uses us as we are, with our differing accents, various educational levels, good and bad grammar, and sometimes even misuse of words that we thought we understood, but did not. An interpretation by a British Oxford University Professor would obviously sound quite different from an interpretation by a South Georgia farmer. However, that which sounds more educated is not necessarily more spiritual. Most of the apostles were "ignorant" Galilean fishermen, but they were among the most spiritual men in history.

We Can Control the Gift

But if there be no interpreter, let him keep silence in the church; and let him speak to himself, and to God (1 Corinthians 14:28).

If there is no one present with the gift of interpretation, it is out of order to speak in tongues. The body would not be edified. They would not know what was said in tongues.

God's command is to keep quiet if there is no interpreter. You can pray in tongues quietly, speaking to yourself, and to God.

It is obvious from these Scriptures that we have control over the gift in that we can choose to speak or not to speak in tongues. I have heard stories about people lying on the floor and speaking uncontrollably in tongues for hours. That contradicts Scripture. We are able to control the gift of tongues, just as we are able to control whether we will speak out in a prophecy. In the next section, we will also see that "the spirits of the prophets are subject to (under the control of) the prophets" (1 Corinthians 14:32).

Scriptural Use of Tongues

Note what we have learned in this section about tongues:

1. Speak to God: We speak to God in tongues (not unto men) (v. 2).

2. Prayer: Tongues is a form of prayer, spiritual prayer: "my spirit prayeth" (v. 14).

3. Blessing: Tongues blesses God with the spirit (v. 16).

4. Thanksgiving: Tongues gives thanks to God (v. 16).

5. Private prayer:

   a. Tongues is primarily for my private prayer life (v. 19).

   b. Private tongues does not have to be interpreted(v. 28).

6. Edification:

   a. Tongues edifies the one speaking in tongues (v. 4).

   b. Tongues edifies others when interpreted (v. 5).

   c. Tongues does not edify the one who does not understand (v. 9).

7. Limited utterances:

   a. In the assembly of believers, only two, or at the most three utterances in tongues are allowed (v. 27).

   b. Only one person should speak at the time (v. 27).

8. Interpretation:

a. Tongues in the assembly must be interpreted (v. 27).

b. If there is no interpreter, then the gift should not be used out loud (v. 28).

c. Those with tongues should pray for the gift of interpretation (v. 13).

The Use of Prophecy in an Assembly

Let the prophets speak two or three, and let the other judge (1 Corinthians 14:29).

As with tongues in an assembly of believers, two or three people may prophesy. The prophecy must then be judged. How do we judge prophecy? What are the criteria that we use? As we already learned, prophecy is God speaking to us.

Judging Prophecy

1. The Word: We judge by the Word of God. There should be no conflict between Scripture and a prophecy today from God. For instance, if someone prophesied that tomorrow there was going be an earthquake in Israel and the Mount of Olives would be destroyed, I would judge that prophecy to be false. Why? Scripture tells us that when

Christ comes back to this earth, He will come to the Mount of Olives. If it was no longer there, Scripture could not be fulfilled.

2. Nature of God: Since a prophecy is God speaking, it should be accordance with the nature of God.

   a. Love: "God is love" (1 John 4:8). A prophecy should reflect the love of God for us, and it should help produce the fruit of love in the life of a believer.

   b. A prophecy should produce faith, and hope for the believer.

   c. It should fulfill 1 Corinthians 14:3: "He that prophesieth speaketh unto men to edification, exhortation, and comfort." It should build us up, stir us up, and cheer us up.

   d. A prophecy should not cause fear for the believer. God is not the author of fear. "For God hath not given us the spirit of fear; but of power, and of love, and of a sound mind" (2 Timothy 1:7).

3. Prediction: If a prophecy from God predicts the future, it must come to pass, according

to Deuteronomy. "When a prophet speaketh in the name of the LORD, if the thing follow not, nor come to pass, that is the thing which the LORD hath not spoken" (Deuteronomy 18:22). Most prophecies today are not predictive. Most are given as encouragement to the believers.

4. Discernment as a body: My spirit bears witness. "The Spirit itself beareth witness with our spirit" (Romans 8:16). What does the body of believers witness regarding the prophecy?

    Who are the ones to judge? The one God is using to conduct the meeting has the primary responsibility to judge. If other elders, deacons, or church leaders are present, they also may help in judging prophecy.

Prophecy Concerning Calvary Chapel

Prophecies are occasionally predictive, and it can be very exciting when they are fulfilled. For instance, Pastor Chuck Smith has mentioned a prophecy that was given in the early days of Calvary Chapel when he was still considering whether or not to become their pastor. Someone prophesied that he would agree to come as their pastor, that he would make certain changes in the sanctuary, that they would later meet in a church overlooking the Bay in Newport Beach, and that Calvary Chapel would become known all over the world. When he agreed to come and then suggested certain changes in the sanctuary, they got very excited. He thought, "What an enthusiastic group." Only later did he find out about the prophecy and the reason for their excitement. Pastor Chuck and the body at Calvary Chapel have watched each of these portions of the prophecy come true over the years. It has been very exciting to see it fulfilled, and to be a part of it.

A False Prophecy

Remember the prophecy I mentioned earlier about a great earthquake and the town being destroyed? That actually happened at Calvary Chapel Costa Mesa. Someone gave this prophecy in a Believer's Meeting. It caused a rush of fear to go through those present. I pronounced it false, as not being in accordance with the nature of God and with 1 Corinthians 14:3. It brought fear, not comfort. When you judge a prophecy to be false, there will be those who will get upset with you, as some did with me that night. But if we are to allow the gift to operate in an assembly of the believers, we must do it in accordance with Scripture, and judge. False prophecies are not a common occurrence, at least not at Calvary Chapels, but we should be prepared for them if we lead Believer's Meetings. Almost all the prophecies I have heard at Calvary Chapels have been uplifting, beautiful words of encouragement from God.

> *If any thing be revealed to another that sitteth by,*
> *let the first hold his peace (1 Corinthians 14:30).*

One person should not monopolize the use of this gift. If another receives a prophecy from God, the first one should be quiet, and let him speak.

The Gift of Prophecy and the Office of a Prophet

> *For ye may all prophesy one by one, that all may*
> *learn, and all may be comforted (1 Corinthians*
> *14:31).*

Prophecy is a gift that most believers can receive, and use to minister to others. Since this gift is available to us, and if we have the gift, we "may all prophesy" (1 Corinthians 14:31), does that make us all prophets? There is a distinction in Scripture between the *gift* of prophecy, and the *office* of a prophet.

All prophets have the gift of prophecy, but not all believers who have the gift of prophecy, are prophets. A prophet is a person, ordained by God, to the office, or position of a prophet. They are second in authority in the church, after apostles. "God hath set some in the church, first apostles, secondarily prophets" (1 Corinthians 12:28). Agabus was a New Testament prophet who prophesied concerning the future imprisonment of Paul (Acts 21:10–11), and a famine, which "came to pass in the days of Claudius Caesar" (Acts 11:28). The office of a prophet is a gift by God to the church (Ephesians 4:11). It is a person with a special calling by God, whereas the gift of prophecy is available to nearly all of us.

And the spirits of the prophets are subject to the prophets (1 Corinthians 14:32).

The prophet is able to control himself, and control when he speaks, and when he does not speak. God does not grab him and throw him down on the floor and make him do strange things. He is not called to interrupt the pastor's sermon. He is not called to draw attention to himself. He is called to exercise the gifts, including prophecy, in love. He is called to strengthen, encourage, and build up the body of Christ, and to help them know Jesus in a deeper, more intimate way. Like John the Baptist, the true prophet knows that "He (Jesus) must increase, I (the prophet) must decrease" (John 3:30).

> *For God is not the author of confusion, but of peace, as in all churches of the saints (1 Corinthians 14:33).*

This speaks volumes. If there is confusion in a church in the use of the gifts, God is not causing it. Satan and man bring confusion and strife, but God brings peace in the churches.

> *Wherefore, brethren, covet to prophesy, and forbid not to speak with tongues (1 Corinthians 14:39).*

He said earlier to covet the best gifts, and prophecy is one of the best, and better than tongues. But we are not to forbid others to speak in tongues, we are to use tongues properly in the assembly. We should encourage the use of tongues, especially in our private prayer lives.

Let all things be done decently and in order (1 Corinthians 14:40).

This is a key verse, which summarizes much of Paul's teaching in this chapter. God wants our meetings, our lives, all things to be done decently and in order.

The Proper Use of the Gifts Leads to Evangelism

Moreover, brethren, I declare unto you the gospel which I preached unto you, which also ye have received, and wherein ye stand;

By which also ye are saved, if ye keep in memory what I preached unto you, unless ye have believed in vain (1 Corinthians 15:1–2).

Immediately after the instruction in the use of the gifts of the Holy Spirit in 1 Corinthians 12–14, Paul begins to talk about the gospel and evangelism in chapter fifteen. This is the natural and supernatural result of doing all things decently and in order, according to the Word of God. We are saved by the gospel, the good news of Jesus Christ. We must hold firmly to the Word, otherwise our faith is superficial and not a saving faith.

For I delivered unto you first of all that which I also received, how that Christ died for our sins according to the scriptures;

And that he was buried, and that he rose again the third day according to the scriptures (1 Corinthians 15:3–4).

These two verses are one of the most succinct statements of the gospel in Scripture. The purpose of the baptism of the Holy Spirit is that we might "be witnesses" unto him. The gifts empower us to be His witnesses and minister to one another and the unsaved. The result is worship of Him, fellowship with Him and one another, and the evangelization of the world. This is what the gospel is all about.

CHAPTER 4

THE BELIEVER'S MEETING

How to Conduct a Believer's Meeting With the Proper Use of the Gifts

As mentioned before, the scriptural basis for a Believer's Meeting is found in 1 Corinthians 14:26.

> *How is it then, brethren? When ye come together, every one of you hath a **psalm**, hath a **doctrine**, hath a **tongue**, hath a **revelation**, hath an **interpretation**. Let all things be done unto edifying (1 Corinthians 14:26, emphasis added).*

When the believers gather together, these are the kinds of things we should expect to happen. Most churches have unbelievers and those who are untaught in the use of the gifts of the Holy Spirit attending their general services.

113

Since it would be unscriptural to expose them to the use of tongues in a general service, a Believer's Meeting is the proper place for the service mentioned in 1 Corinthians 14:26.

At the beginning of the meeting, I read 1 Corinthians 14:26 and tell the people that this Scripture is the basis for our meeting.

What are we to expect in our meeting?

1. Psalm(s)—Singing unto the Lord. A time of worship and praise.

2. Doctrine—Teaching of the Word.

If we have "Believer's Meetings" infrequently, the teaching will usually center around the baptism of the Holy Spirit and the gifts of the Spirit and their proper use. Believers who are "unlearned" in the gifts will then better understand their use in the meeting. If "Believer's Meetings" are conducted frequently, then the teaching of any portion of God's Word is appropriate. A brief mention of the use of the gifts may still be in order for the new ones present.

3. Tongues—the use of tongues is appropriate in the meeting.

The use of tongues is restricted to a particular time in the service. Tongues should never interrupt the teaching of the Word. The gift of teaching is also the operation of a gift of the Holy Spirit. Speaking out in tongues when someone is teaching the Word is not only unscriptural, but rude. If the Holy Spirit is ministering through the gift of teaching, why would he have someone interrupt him with a tongue? As Pastor Chuck Smith says, "The Holy Spirit is a gentleman, and he does not interrupt himself."

The time for tongues is when the leader tells the flock that the use of tongues is now appropriate in the meeting. Tongues is a restricted gift, at the most only two or three should speak, one after the other, and someone should interpret (1 Corinthians 14:27).

4. Revelation—Supernatural information from God.

This could be the use of a number of gifts, such as word of wisdom, word of knowledge, discerning of spirits, or prophecy. In the "revelation" gifts, God reveals something to the believer supernaturally, something he could not have known otherwise. Once we receive a revelation, we have several options:

a. God may want us to reveal what He has shown us to the body of believers. If we speak to others a revelation from God, then what we speak is prophecy. We are speaking forth what God has spoken to us. Remember, prophecy is God speaking to His people. A word from God, be it word of wisdom, word of knowledge, or discerning of spirits, when spoken to us, becomes prophecy. We can then apply the test of a prophecy to what is spoken. It should be in accordance with Scripture. It should edify us (build us up), exhort us (stir us up), and comfort us (cheer us up) (1 Corinthians 14:3). We also should learn something from a prophecy (1 Corinthians 14:31), though it is not the same as the gift of teaching.

b. God may want us to speak to an individual in private about what He has revealed.

c. God may reveal something to us so that we will pray for a person or a particular situation. God may not call us to speak what He has revealed.

As in tongues, two or three prophets should speak, one at the time, and the prophecies should be judged.

When I am conducting a meeting, I often ask those with the gift of prophecy to raise their hands. If I know those with the gift and I am familiar with their ministry of the gift, I feel more secure in inviting them to prophesy. Someone unfamiliar to me certainly may also prophesy. It is a good idea to let them know in advance that we judge prophecies according to Scripture.

5. Interpretation—Interpretation of Tongues.

When tongues are used, they must be accompanied by an interpretation of the tongue. With an interpretation, the body of believers will know what was said to the Lord, and be edified.

Therefore, when you have tongues in a meeting, someone with the gift of interpretation must be present who is willing to give the interpretation.

When I am conducting a meeting, I sometimes ask those present with the gift of interpretation to raise their hands. Then I know that if someone speaks in tongues, others can interpret. I also have the gift of interpretation.

If you are conducting a meeting and you do not have the gift of interpretation and no one else present does, then it is unscriptural to have tongues in the meeting. Tongues should be omitted.

Some Practical Ideas: "Nuts and Bolts" of a Believer's Meeting

1. Many pastors like to have a couple of microphones placed in the congregation so that those who speak in tongues, prophesy, or interpret tongues can be heard. This would especially be valuable in a large church. However, someone needs to control the microphones so that they can be turned off with a signal from the leader if someone gets out of control, and starts to say ungodly or unscriptural things.

2. Large meetings may be unwieldy. If there are several hundred people present, it may be difficult to let many exercise their gifts.

3. Don't be too rigid. People learning to use the gifts are going to make honest mistakes.

Correct them gently and in love. However if you discern that someone has an unscriptural agenda in their use of the gifts, more forceful correction may be needed. Generally try to avoid direct confrontation in the meeting if possible. Use Scripture to correct error. After correction, you might say something like, "Let's discuss it after the meeting," and then move on.

4. Pray for the body that God will give others the boldness to step out in faith and use their gifts. Remind them that Paul told Timothy, "Stir up the gift of God, which is in thee by the putting (laying) on of my hands" (2 Timothy 1:6). You don't want the meeting to be a "one-man show." The use of the gifts is to be a body ministry, but as the leader, God has called you to be an example to the believers in the use of the gifts.

5. As the leader, you set the tone and direction for the meeting under the guidance of the Holy Spirit. Remember the "Motivational Gifts" mentioned previously? If your main gift is teaching, you will probably really delve into what the Word has to say about the baptism and the gifts. If your main gift is

prophecy, you will probably spend more time in the meeting with prophetic utterances that are designed to "build up, stir up, and cheer" up the church. If your gift is mercy, you will be concerned about using the gifts to minister to broken hearts. No matter what your gifts, however, the main emphasis should always be on Christ: who He is, what He has done for us, and how much He loves us.

6. Always be flexible. Not every Believer's Meeting is the same. One you conduct may be totally different from the one another leader conducts. And the one you do tonight will not be the same as the one last week. The Holy Spirit wants to express the personality of Jesus Christ and minister to the needs of the body present. So the best way we can lead a meeting is to give control over to the Holy Spirit and let Him have His way. Interestingly enough, this requires that we strictly control the meeting to make sure that we stay within scriptural guidelines. We don't want to quench the Spirit by disobeying His Word. Be totally familiar with the teaching of 1 Corinthians chapter

fourteen. Obey Scripture, wait on the Lord, love His people, and He will minister.

7. Don't try to "make it happen." Sometimes, when I open up the meeting to the use of the vocal gifts in the afterglow, no one says anything. Don't be embarrassed by periods of silence. Sometimes God waits before He speaks. Sometimes God has given someone something to speak, but they are hesitant, afraid they will say the wrong thing. If I have an impression from God that He wants someone to speak who is hesitant, I will gently encourage them by saying something like, "God has given someone a prophecy and He wants you to know it is from Him; that you can speak it out to us without fear." Then I wait a little longer. Usually they will speak out. If they still do not speak, I move on in the meeting. Generally, the Holy Spirit will give me the same prophecy and I will speak it to the people. When I give a prophecy, often people will come up to me after the service and tell me that God had spoken something similar to them, but they were afraid to speak. I encourage them to speak up in our next meeting when they receive similar words from God.

8. If God does not seem to be speaking to you
    or to others, pray that He will show you
    what He wants to do in the meeting. He
    may want you to have a healing service and
    anoint people with oil for prayer. He may
    want the body to have a time of repentance
    before Him. He may want a Worship and
    Praise service. He may want you to end the
    meeting early. Be flexible. Again, don't try
    to "make it happen," or force God to do
    things, or force people in the use of the gifts.
    Don't feel pressured. Don't get the idea that
    your "reputation" as a leader of Believer's
    Meetings is on the line. Flow with the Spirit.
    Worship, love the Lord, love His people,
    and He will "make it happen."

9. Last year I attended a meeting of Calvary
    Chapel pastors in which Pastor Brian
    Brodersen led an Afterglow Service. Brian
    has led many Afterglows. I was anticipating
    powerful prophecies from these men of
    God. But God did not give any prophecies.
    No one spoke. I usually receive prophecies
    in meetings I am leading, but I did not
    receive one in Brian's meeting. God, in His
    providence, had no prophecies at that
    meeting. Brian wisely moved on in the

service and had prayer for healing of the sick. That was what God wanted that night. Brian followed the leading of the Holy Spirit. God does not always do what we expect. Again, be flexible.

What Should Be the Result of a Believer's Meeting?

Through the baptism and the gifts of the Holy Spirit, we can have a miraculous encounter with the true and living God. All of the activities in the meeting should help us to know Jesus in a deeper, more intimate way. They should make us realize how much God loves us, and that He speaks to us today, understands us, and is concerned about us. They should make us more loving, more Christ-like. We should leave the meeting built up in the faith, stirred up into Spirit-led action for Him, and comforted in His great love for us. We should have a reverential awe of His power and greatness, and His ability to heal us.

On the negative side, we should not leave the meeting overawed by the forceful, dynamic personality of the leader, thinking he is some great one. We should not leave feeling inferior to others because they had impressive, showy gifts of the Spirit. We should not leave confused about unscriptural practices such as people falling down, being "slain in the Spirit," speaking uncontrollably in tongues, running up and down the aisles of the church, jumping over pews, barking like dogs, or roaring like lions. These unscriptural practices cater to the flesh, do not edify the body of Christ, and do not glorify Jesus Christ.

First Corinthians 14:26 is our basic Scripture for conducting the meeting, but many others amplify our activities.

And be not drunk with wine, wherein is excess; but be filled with the Spirit: Speaking to yourselves in psalms and hymns and spiritual songs, singing and making melody in your heart to the Lord (Ephesians 5:18–19).

Let the word of Christ dwell in you richly in all wisdom; teaching and admonishing one another in psalms and hymns and spiritual songs, singing with grace in your hearts to the Lord (Colossians 3:16).

These two similar Scriptures apply to our everyday walk with the Lord as well as a "Believer's Meeting." The Scriptures must be our guide if we want to obey God and be pleasing to

Him. Unscriptural practices quench or grieve the Spirit. All of 1 Corinthians chapter fourteen is dedicated to the proper use of the spoken gifts, not only in a "Believer's Meeting," but in our everyday lives, moment by moment.

Practical Application
An Example of a "Believer's Meeting"

1. Singing—worship and praise.

2. Doctrine—Teaching the Word. Read 1 Corinthians 14:26. Brief explanation of the difference between a regular service and a "Believer's Meeting."

3. *Prayer* for those present who would like to receive the *baptism of the Holy Spirit*. I ask that anyone who wants prayer for the baptism of the Holy Spirit to come forward for prayer. We lay hands on them to pray for them to receive the baptism of the Holy Spirit. "When Paul had laid his hands upon them, the Holy Ghost came on them; and they spake with tongues, and prophesied" (Acts 19:6).

   If we have a large group come forward to receive, I have several elders and deacons come forward to help me pray for the people and lay hands on them. During this time, the musicians at Calvary Chapel Tallahassee, often play or sing softly in the background while we are praying for people. I ask the body of believers present to pray for us and those who are receiving.

4. *Prayer* for those present who would like to receive gifts of the Holy Spirit.

    As above, I ask for those who want to receive gifts of the Holy Spirit to come forward for prayer. We lay hands on them to pray for them to receive the gifts. "Neglect not the gift that is in thee, which was given thee by prophecy, with the laying on of the hands of the presbytery (elders)" (1 Timothy 4:14).

    The elders and deacons help me. Musicians may play. Again, I often ask the congregation to pray for us.

5. **Afterglow:** Operation of the gifts of the Spirit in the service:

    Next I invite the people to minister to one another and to the Lord in the gifts of the Spirit in the meeting. This part of the service is done in an attitude of prayer. I will pray and ask God to speak to us, through us, and minister to us. If the people are hesitant, I will generally step out in faith and speak in tongues. Someone else may interpret, but if they do not, I interpret my own tongue. God will give us the interpretation because it would be unscriptural not to have one. I encourage those with the gift of tongues or prophecy to speak out. Patience is required. Do not be embarrassed by silence. Wait on the Lord. Many times we are very aware of the presence of the Lord during times of silence. Frequently people will weep softly as God is touching their hearts. Musicians may quietly play and sing or we may have total silence while we are waiting for God to speak to us.

a. Spoken gifts: The spoken gifts may alternate. We might have someone speak in tongues, then an interpretation, then a prophecy, then another tongue, followed by an interpretation.

   i. Tongues—two or three.

ii. Interpretation of tongues. Each utterance in tongues should be followed by its interpretation.

iii. Prophecy—two or three people may speak and each statement must be judged. After someone speaks, I will usually make a comment such as, "Praise the Lord for that beautiful prophecy." In this way, I can judge it without announcing that I am doing so.

   1) Edification, Exhortation, Comfort. Most of the prophecies will usually fit in this category, with God speaking to us through one of His vessels to build us up, stir us up, or cheer us up.

   2) Revelation gifts:

      a) Word of knowledge

      b) Word of wisdom

      c) Discerning of spirits

I included the revelation gifts under prophecy because when a revelation from God is spoken, it becomes prophecy.

If God tells you something which you then speak forth in the meeting, you are speaking the word God gave you. Thus it becomes prophecy when you speak it.

Word of knowledge: these might be about illnesses, family problems, financial problems, anything in which someone needs a touch from God. Word of knowledge is often used by the Lord for healing. God may tell me or someone else that someone present has a sore throat, a sinus infection, heart trouble, depression, or any of a number of problems. If the word of knowledge is that He is healing them, I tell them to be sure to go to their doctor for confirmation if it is a serious problem. If a healing is real, it will bear up under medical scrutiny. We should be as "wise as serpents, and harmless as doves" (Matthew 10:16). I never tell people to go off their medicine such as insulin unless it is with the approval and under the direction of their doctor. If cancer is healed, God will confirm the healing through the patient's doctor. Modern medicine is not the enemy of the miraculous, but should substantiate it. At a Believer's Meeting in 1996, the Lord gave me the word of knowledge that someone there had cancer, and that He was going to be with her, and heal her. Part of the word was that she should see a physician. She was healed through surgery in this case. (Also see section on word of knowledge.)

Word of wisdom: these might be warnings from God, a word about how to handle a tough situation at home or at work, direction for someone's life, or any of a number of situations in which God's wisdom is needed. Word of wisdom and word of knowledge often work together. Through word of knowledge, God may tell someone something is wrong, and through word of wisdom, He may tell someone else what should be done about it. (Also see section on word of wisdom.)

Discerning of spirits: used to discern what is from the Lord, and what is not. This gift is needed to discern false prophets and false teachers. At one Believer's meeting, I discerned that a man was demon possessed. The Lord had me say publicly that someone in the meeting was demon possessed, but that if he would renounce Satan in his heart, Christ would come in and he would be saved. He did, and was born again that night. (Also see section on discernment of spirits.)

    b.   Power gifts:

    i.   Gift(s) of healing(s)

    ii.   Gift of faith

    iii. Working of miracles

Occasionally the "power gifts" will be manifested. I have had many people tell me over the years that they received a healing at a Believer's Meeting. This has happened through the word of knowledge, and through the laying on of hands as in James 5:14–15. One night at a Believer's Meeting in Costa Mesa, a girl fell down on the floor during the service, and started making awful facial grimaces, and animal-like noises. We discerned that she was demon-possessed, prayed for her, and the demon was cast out through the gift of faith. She accepted Jesus Christ as her Savior right there, and our meeting became a celebration of joy for God's marvelous work of deliverance, and salvation. (See also the section on the "Power Gifts.")

    c.   Other gifts: exhortation, mercy, giving. Any of the other gifts may be in operation and manifested.

6. Prayer for Healing of the sick (James 5:14–15). Take oil to anoint them for the

prayer of faith. Many times people come to a Believer's meeting needing a healing. Because the power of God is being manifested supernaturally, I encourage people to receive a healing from the Lord.

An Example of an Afterglow Service

An example outline for an Afterglow Service is similar to a Believer's Meeting, but the "doctrinal" portion is very brief since doctrine has been taught in the regular church service. I usually start an Afterglow Service with a few worshipful songs about Jesus and the Holy Spirit. Some comments about the baptism of the Holy Spirit and the proper use of the gifts are in order. I then invite those present to receive the baptism and the gifts of the Holy Spirit. After the laying on of hands and prayer for this group, I invite the believers to exercise the gifts as in the Afterglow Service of a Believer's Meeting, outlined in the previous section.

The service may be brief, only lasting twenty to thirty minutes, or it may be longer. The Holy Spirit ministers in many different ways. These are only a few suggestions. As before, the key is to do things decently and in order, in a worshipful manner, honoring the Lord.

How the Gifts of Prophecy and Tongues Can Work Together in a Believer's Meeting

One night several years ago in a Believer's Meeting at Calvary Chapel Costa Mesa, something very beautiful happened that demonstrates how the gifts of the Spirit can work together and complement one another. We were having a quiet time, waiting on the Lord. John Ezell, one of the elders, gave a beautiful prophecy from the Song of Solomon. Then a lady spoke in tongues. The Lord gave me the interpretation of her tongue.

Putting it all together, it went like this:

PROPHECY:

Rise up, my love, my fair one, and come away.

For lo, the winter is past,

the rain is over and gone.

The flowers appear on the earth;

the time of the singing of birds has come,

and the voice of the turtledove

is heard in our land.

Arise, my love, my fair one, and come away.

TONGUE:

******

INTERPRETATION:

Oh my Lord, my master, my savior, my love.

I worship you and I adore you,

for you are my most high God.

Beside you, there is no other.

I arise, I come to you,

I give myself to you, my love.

I long for the day when you return

to take me away to be with you forever.

As the deer longs for the water of the waterbrook,

so my soul longs for you,

my savior, my Lord, and my God.

A beautiful hush fell over the body of Christ that night as these words were spoken. As in the Song of Solomon, the bridegroom spoke (prophecy from the Lord to His bride, the church). Then the bride responded (tongues, followed by the interpretation, in which the bride speaks to the bridegroom). This example is consistent with the teaching of 1 Corinthians chapter fourteen. In prophecy, the Lord (the bridegroom) speaks to the church. In tongues, the church (the bride) speaks (responds) to the Lord.

CHAPTER 5
A FINAL WORD

The Supernatural Realm

As Christians we hunger in our hearts to experience the supernatural work of God. Exciting things are mentioned in the Scriptures, such as healings, prophecies, the working of miracles. While we desire to see these things, we are often afraid and skeptical because we have seen so much abuse of the gifts of the Holy Spirit in the church. Unscriptural use of the gifts, phony faith healers, false teachers, and false prophets are all things which concern us and make us hesitant to enter into that realm, and perhaps a little skeptical of those who do. But where there is a counterfeit, there is also the genuine article. God wants us to enter in to all the fullness of the Spirit.

God's Word Is Our Guide

We can rest assured that the Word of God has given us all we need to know to enter into the supernatural realm with confidence and assurance. But we must always remember that the Scriptures are to be our guide. They must be the yardstick by which we measure the supernatural realm, and our supernatural experiences. If someone performs a miracle and does not give the glory to Jesus Christ, then we should have nothing to do with that person or that ministry. The Scriptures tell us that even Satan can perform miracles. Satan's false prophet will be able to call fire down from heaven in Revelation 13:13. We should not be impressed by miracles alone, but should ask, "Is Jesus Christ being glorified?" "Is what happened in accordance with the Word of God?"

We Already Have Access Through Prayer

We already have access into the supernatural realm through prayer. One problem with most of our prayers is that we give God a shopping list of things we want Him to do and then say, "Amen," and never wait for God to speak to us. We like to do all the talking. In my personal prayer time, I have a note to myself at the end for a "Quiet time," to listen to God. I stop speaking, and wait, and listen to God for a few minutes. During this time, the Lord speaks to me. It may be very short, just a few words or an impression from the Lord of encouragement about the upcoming events of the day, and the sorts of things that I will encounter that day. He may speak to my heart about some concern for which I have been praying, or I may sense His abiding presence and love. Part of our problem is we just do not take time to stop and listen. We want to rush through our prayer life the same way we rush through everything else in our modern day society.

I have listed a prayer outline below, which I use and have found very valuable. I got this from Bible teacher, Chuck Missler. However, I have added to it my "Quiet time" of listening to God, and my prayer time in tongues. If I forget to pray for something in English, I trust the Holy Spirit to pray through me in my prayer language to the Father for anything I

overlooked. For those who do not have a prayer
language, Paul tells us in Romans 8:26, that we
can pray in the spirit with "groanings that
cannot be uttered." Sometimes I just groan in
prayer.

Prayer Outline

1.Worship (including praise and thanksgiving)
2. Repentance
3. Petitions
4. Intercessions
5. Quiet Time—Listen to God
6. Pray in Tongues
7. Worship

Commonly Asked Questions

1.   **Question:** I heard about a lady from another
country who spoke a foreign language. She
heard someone speaking in tongues. She said
they were speaking to her in her language. They
gave her directions and a very beautiful
message from God. What was happening?

Answer: Those who teach that tongues can
be used to give a message to the church use this
story as an example. 1 Corinthians 14:2 tells us
"he that speaketh in an unknown tongue
speaketh not unto men, but unto God."

Therefore when we speak in tongues, we are speaking to God. What happened?

We know that God can speak to people through supernatural means. He spoke to Balaam through a donkey. Certainly God could speak to someone through another person in a foreign language. Then, it would not be the usual gift of speaking in tongues, but would be a *miracle* from God.

We must be very careful that we do not formulate doctrine based on our experiences. This lady's experience seems to indicate that tongues speaks to men, but the Scriptures say otherwise. We must interpret her experience from the Scriptures. If this was a valid experience from God, then it must be a miracle. If we use our experiences to interpret Scripture, then we might conclude that tongues could be used to give us a message. Then we would get confused about what constitutes an interpretation of a tongue. The Scriptures must be the standard, not our experiences.

2. **Question:** What about being "slain in the spirit" in Believers Services?

Answer: There is no reference in the New Testament of a believer being "slain in the spirit" during a service or at any other time. It is unscriptural, and we should not do it!

Unfortunately some churches make a big show of people falling down and being "slain in the spirit" in their services. 1 Corinthians 14:26 tells us how to conduct a meeting of the believers and the things that should happen when the believers meet together. It does not mention being slain in the spirit. Some use the incident in John chapter eighteen to teach that being slain in the spirit is a valid New Testament experience. In John 18, the *enemies* of Jesus came to take him. Jesus asked, "Whom seek ye?" They answered, "Jesus of Nazareth." He said unto them, "I am." When he said "I am," they went backward, and fell to the ground. But these were the enemies of Christ, not believers.

Comment: I have seen repeatedly that unscriptural practices such as being "slain in the spirit," bring attention and glory to man and to the flesh, rather than to Jesus Christ. It troubles me that people often want to do unscriptural things in a service, when there are so many scriptural things we could and should be doing that are neglected.

3. **Question:** How can I be sure I'm on solid scriptural ground when I exercise the gifts of the Spirit?

Answer: Whatever is scriptural is an acceptable practice. Some doctrines, though, are more important than others. The most important doctrines are taught in three places in the New Testament:

1. They are mentioned in the gospels.

2. They occur in the book of Acts, at the hands of the apostles.

3. They are systematically taught in the epistles.

These are the teachings and the practices that we should most heartily embrace and pursue as Christians. For example, the gospel of Mark said believers would speak in tongues. In Acts, tongues was a manifestation of the baptism of the Holy Spirit at Pentecost. Tongues occurred several other times in Acts (Acts 10, Acts 19). Finally, in his first epistle to the Corinthians, Paul teaches us in detail about tongues in the fourteenth chapter. Therefore, the use of tongues is scriptural, and encouraged, but we must obey the scriptural guidelines as taught in 1 Corinthians chapter fourteen, for the best and proper use of this gift.

4. **Question:** If I am conducting a Believer's Meeting and after three utterances in tongues, a fourth person speaks in tongues, what should I do?

Answer: First, do not get upset. It is not a major blunder. We are not legalists. I tell the believers that the Bible instructs us that we should only have three utterances in tongues in the meeting. Since this was the fourth time, we should not speak out loud in tongues any more. Be gentle with God's sheep. Do not embarrass someone who makes a mistake.

Other pastors have told me they just do not interpret the fourth tongue. That is one possible way to handle it, but if the sheep do not get the message, others may still speak in tongues. Be sensitive to the leading of the Holy Spirit. He will show you ways to handle it.

5. **Question:** What should I do if someone gives a false prophecy?

Answer: If you are conducting the meeting, you must judge the prophecy. The criteria for judging were mentioned in the section on 1 Corinthians chapter fourteen. If the prophecy does not meet the criteria, I say, "That prophecy is not from the Lord." Then I tell why.

If a prophecy is not from the Lord, where is it from? There are three possible sources for prophecy. A true prophecy is from God. A false prophecy may be from Satan, or it may come from the heart of man. Some people may want to prophesy so much that they speak before the Lord has given them anything to speak. Others have a need to be recognized and want to appear spiritual. This type person may give a "prophecy" out of his own heart for these reasons. It is not designed to deceive the body, but its purpose is to draw attention to the one giving the prophecy. I try to be gentle with these two groups, especially the first. I explain that it is possible for us to get ahead of the Lord in our enthusiasm to speak, and we need to wait patiently on Him to give us a prophecy. I review the criteria for a true prophecy. I keep in mind the admonition of Paul,

> *Brethren, if a man be overtaken in a fault, ye*
> *which are spiritual, restore such an one in the*
> *spirit of meekness, considering thyself, lest thou*
> *also be tempted (Galatians 6:1).*

If I know the prophecy is satanic, I do not let them down so easily. I say the prophecy is not from the Lord, and tell why. What happens next depends mostly on the response of the one who gave the prophecy. If he keeps quiet, that may be the end of the matter. If he makes a scene, and challenges the judgment that the prophecy is not from God, I pray that God will give me His wisdom to say what He wants me to say. Once in a Believer's Meeting when I was teaching about the deity of Christ, a lady challenged me. She asked, "Does Chuck Smith know you are teaching that? He doesn't teach that. You're teaching false doctrine!" Instead of defending myself, or appealing to the authority of Pastor Chuck, the Lord had me quote John 1:1, "In the beginning was the Word, and the Word was with God, and the Word was God." I said, "Jesus is the Word. Jesus is God." The Word of God stopped her. She had nothing else to say.

A false prophet of Satan will have a satanic agenda. He will try to get you to put your faith and your trust in something (anything) other than Christ, and Christ alone. Much of what he prophesies may be true, but that which leads you away from a complete trust in Christ is the dangerous part. Some false prophets might try to create fear in your heart. We are not ignorant of Satan's devices, and he will use any of them to try to mislead us. We have the Spirit of Christ, the Holy Spirit to watch over us, protect us, and lead us into all truth. We need not fear.

What do we do with a false prophet? They were commanded to stone them in the Old Testament Scriptures. The Christians did not do that in New Testament times, and we do not today. Paul said,

> *Now I beseech you, brethren, mark them which cause divisions and offences contrary to the doctrine which ye have learned; and avoid them (Romans 16:17).*

We should not hesitate to ask them to leave. Our first duty is to the flock of God, and their protection. Most churches are too timid in this area today. We have no "Christian duty" to put up with disruptive behavior, false teachers, or false prophets. Such should be ushered out of the church, and told not to return. If true repentance takes place, as it did with the man at Corinth that Paul said to put out of the Church (1 Corinthians 5:11), then receive them back, as Paul did. The Apostle Paul did not hesitate to rebuke, exhort, and chastise, all in the name of, and in the love of Jesus Christ.

> *For God is not the author of confusion, but of peace, as in all churches of the saints (1 Corinthians 14:33).*

> *Finally, brethren, whatsoever things are true, whatsoever things are honest, whatsoever things are just, whatsoever things are pure, whatsoever things are lovely, whatsoever things are of good report; if there be any virtue, and if there be any praise, think on these things (Philippians 4:8).*

> *Now unto him that is able to keep you from falling, and to present you faultless before the presence of his glory with exceeding joy, to the only wise God our Savior, be glory and majesty, dominion and power, both now and ever. Amen (Jude 24–25).*

How to Become a Christian

First of all you must recognize that you are a sinner. Realize that you have missed the mark. This is true of each of us. We have deliberately crossed the line not once, but many times. The Bible says, *"All have sinned and fallen short of the glory of God"* (Romans 3:23). This is a hard admission for many to make, but if we are not willing to hear the bad news, we cannot appreciate and respond to the *good news*.

Second, we must realize that Jesus Christ died on the cross for us. Because of sin, God had to take drastic measures to reach us. So He came to this earth and walked here as a man. But Jesus was more than just a good man. He was the God-man—God incarnate—and that is why His death on the cross is so significant.

At the cross, God Himself—in the person of Jesus Christ—took our place and bore our sins. He paid for them and purchased our redemption.

Third, we must repent of our sin. God has commanded men everywhere to repent. Acts 3:19 states, *"Repent therefore and be converted, that your sins may be blotted out, so that times of refreshing may come from the presence of the Lord."* What does this word *repent* mean? It means to change direction–to hang a U-turn on the road of life. It means to stop living the kind of life we led previously and start living the kind of life outlined in the pages of the Bible. Now we must change and be willing to make a break with the past.

Fourth, we must receive Jesus Christ into our hearts and lives. Being a Christian is having God Himself take residence in our lives. John 1:12 tells us, *"But as many as received Him, to them He gave the right to become children of God."* We must receive Him. Jesus said, *"Behold, I stand at the door and knock. If anyone hears My voice and opens the door, I will come in..."* (Revelation 3:20). Each one of us must individually decide to open the door. How do we open it? Through prayer.

If you have never asked Jesus Christ to come into your life, you can do it right now. Here is a suggested prayer you might even pray.

Lord Jesus, I know that I am a sinner and I am sorry for my sin. I turn and repent of my sins right now. Thank You for dying on the cross for me and paying the price for my sin. Please come into my heart and life right now. Fill me with Your Holy Spirit and help me to be Your disciple. Thank You for forgiving me and coming into my life. Thank You that I am now a child of Yours and that I am going to heaven. In Jesus' name, I pray. Amen.

When you pray that prayer God will respond. You have made the right decision–the decision that will impact how you spend eternity. Now you will go to heaven, and in the meantime, find peace and the answers to your spiritual questions.

Taken from: *Life. Any Questions?*

by Greg Laurie, Copyright © 1995. Used by permission.

Other books available in this series...

Spiritual Warfare
by Brian Brodersen
Pastor Brian Brodersen of Calvary Chapel Westminster, England brings biblical balance and practical insight to the subject of spiritual warfare.

Christian Leadership
by Larry Taylor
Pastor Larry Taylor of the Cornerstone Christian Fellowship in Maui, Hawaii discusses the basics of leadership in the church and challenges us to become leaders that serve.

The Psychologizing of the Faith
by Bob Hoekstra
Pastor Bob Hoekstra of Living in Christ Ministries calls the church to leave the broken cisterns of human wisdom, and to return to the fountain of living water flowing from our wonderful counselor, Jesus Christ.

Practical Christian Living
by Wayne Taylor
Pastor Wayne Taylor of Calvary Fellowship in Seattle, Washington takes us through a study of Romans 12 and 13 showing us what practical Christian living is all about.

Building Godly Character
by Ray Bentley
Pastor Ray Bentley of Maranatha Chapel in San Diego, California takes us through a study in the life of David to show how God builds His character in our individual lives.

Worship and Music Ministry
by Rick Ryan & Dave Newton
Pastor Rick Ryan and Dave Newton of Calvary Chapel Santa Barbara, California give us solid biblical insight into the very important subjects of worship and ministering to the body of Christ through music.

Overcoming Sin & Enjoying God
by Danny Bond
Pastor Danny Bond of Pacific Hills Church in Aliso Viejo, California shows us, through practical principles, that it is possible to live in victory over sin and have constant fellowship with our loving God.

Answers for the Skeptic
by Scott Richards
Pastor Scott Richards of Calvary Fellowship in Tucson, Arizona shows us what to say when our faith is challenged, and how to answer the skeptic in a way that opens hearts to the love and truth of Jesus Christ.

Effective Prayer Life
by Chuck Smith
Pastor Chuck Smith of Calvary Chapel of Costa Mesa, California discusses the principles of prayer, the keys to having a dynamic prayer life, and the victorious results of such a life. It will stir in your heart a desire to "pray without ceasing."

Creation by Design
by Mark Eastman, M.D.
Mark Eastman, M.D., of Genesis Outreach in Temecula, California carefully examines and clarifies the evidence for a Creator God, and the reality of His relationship to mankind.

The Afterglow
by Henry Gainey

Pastor Henry Gainey of Calvary Chapel Thomasville, Georgia gives instruction in conducting and understanding the proper use of the gifts of the Holy Spirit in an "Afterglow Service."

Final Curtain
by Chuck Smith

Pastor Chuck Smith of Calvary Chapel Costa Mesa, California provides insight into God's prophetic plan and shows how current events are leading to the time when one climactic battle will usher in eternity.

For ordering information, please contact:
The Word For Today
P.O. Box 8000, Costa Mesa, CA 92628
(800) 272-WORD
Also, visit us on the Internet at:
www.thewordfortoday.org